Faith on the Edge Series

Science
and
the Savior

The Calling of a Scientist

Angus Menuge

CONCORDIA PUBLISHING HOUSE · SAINT LOUIS

Manufactured in United States of America, La Vergne, TN/039505/406884

Written by Angus Menuge

Edited by Edward Engelbrecht

All Scripture quotations are from the HOLY BIBLE, NEW INTERNATIONAL VERSION®. NIV®. Copyright © 1973, 1978, 1984 by International Bible Society. Used by permission of Zondervan Publishing House. All rights reserved.

This publication may be available in braille, in large print, or on cassette tape for the visually impaired. Please allow 8 to 12 weeks for delivery. Write to the Library for the Blind, 1333 S. Kirkwood Road, St. Louis, MO 63122-7295; call 1-800-433-3954, ext. 1322; or e-mail to blind. library@lcms.org.

Manufactured in the United States of America, La Vergne, TN / 039505 / 406884

1 2 3 4 5 6 7 8 9 10   13 12 11 10 09 08 07 06 05 04

CONTENTS

About This Series

In the past, science served as a stepchild of alchemy, a handmaiden of theology, and a tool of industry. At the beginning of the twentieth century, science took on a new role. Science became the answer to all humankind's problems. Scientists pulled on their white lab coats, prophesied through their theories, and consecrated each new discovery or invention. Humans marveled.

In response to these new inventions, a new type of literature arose—science fiction, which sometimes warned us about the maddening pace of technology. The robot would replace the human worker. Nuclear fallout would devastate life on earth. Science would solve people's problems by doing away with people, or at least by doing away with their humanity.

Today, people remain thankful for science. But they also recognize that science does not hold all the answers. In fact, they see that science can raise more questions than it answers, driving people on further quests for understanding, truth, and contentment.

The Faith on the Edge Bible study series tracks the progress of science and people's fascinations and fears about science. Each session introduces a contemporary topic, summarizes what science has to say about it, and then provides biblical answers and guidance so that you can face the future with the wisdom and confidence that only God can provide.

Student Introduction

When we grab our umbrella on the way out the door, we take the advice of a scientist about the weather. When we buy prepackaged food, we buy into someone's research about microbes. When we kick back to enjoy the game, we enjoy the benefits of the latest in telecommunication.

Modern science began as a rare and specialized discipline. Today, science and scientific ideas touch our daily lives and govern numerous types of work. See if you can find your place in the following list:

Aeronautics

Agritech

Anthropology

Archaeology

Astronomy

Biology

Chemistry

Computing

Ecology

Economics

Engineering

Forensics

Genetics

Geology

Immunology

Histology

Kinetics

Manufacturing

Mathematics

Medicine

Meteorology

Nursing

Pharmacology

Physics

Psychology

Robotics

Telecommunications

Transportation

Zoology

Modern science has grown to touch every field of study and every occupation. But amid all this knowledge and technology something is being lost: meaning, morality, and our immortal souls. The children of modern science are in danger of fulfilling the apostle Paul's words, "Although they claimed to be wise, they became fools" (Romans 1:22).

We are learning that knowledge is a poor substitute for goodness. Technology eases some burdens of humanness but aggravates others. No matter how intelligent we grow, we cannot outgrow our weaknesses. Simply put, we never outgrow our need for God.

This study will help you explore some of the issues, facts, and myths about modern science and the Christian faith. It will teach you to appreciate science as a blessing from your Creator. It will also help you see scientists as the great astronomer and mathematician Johannes Kepler saw them, as "priests of the highest God in regard to the book of nature."

The editor

CHAPTER ONE

God's Intentions for Science

Nonreligious people typically see science as something that humans decided to do for themselves without any guidance from God. For them science shows the authority of human reason and rejects God's Word as outmoded superstition. This may be called *autonomous science*. It creates the sense that human beings can figure everything out for themselves, without God's guiding hand.

Nonreligious people see advances in agricultural science and industrial food processing—and not God—as providers of their daily bread. They look to pharmaceuticals, not to God, as the source of healing and health. In effect, they see science as a source of secular salvation, saving us from hard work, pain, and illness by the wonders of technology and medicine. For example, in highly secularized Europe, one could argue that faith in science is more prevalent than faith in God.

1. Reflect on today's fascination and trust in science. Can you think of examples that illustrate "faith" in science?

Faced with this confident rejection of God, Christians sometimes conclude that science is a dangerous thing, since it encourages human beings to play God, supplanting His roles as Provider and Savior.

Some feel tempted to conclude that science was not part of God's intention for human beings. They conclude that science epitomizes the prideful rejection of God's sovereignty and the desire to be "like God" in knowledge and power (Genesis 3:5). In other words, the fact that unbelievers embrace science as a way of rejecting God encourages some believers to reject science.

 2. Read Proverbs 23:12 and 23. Do education and the pursuit of knowledge undermine faith? Why or why not?

 Believers rightly perceive the danger that science can become a tower of Babel (Genesis 11) and that faith in human ingenuity and power over the natural world can supplant faith in the Creator and Savior of that world. However, we must not fail to consider the idea that God can have different and better intentions for science.

Autonomy and Humility

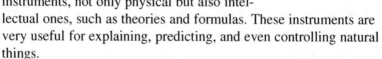

E xcessive confidence in science reflects a misunderstanding of what science is. Ultimately science provides a collection of instruments, not only physical but also intellectual ones, such as theories and formulas. These instruments are very useful for explaining, predicting, and even controlling natural things.

 But first, it should be noted that something can be useful without being true. A scientific theory can make the right predictions without being an accurate model of reality. For example, in about A.D. 150 the Egyptian scientist Ptolemy wrote his *Almagest,* which provided an ingenious method for computing the orbits of the known planets. The model assumed that all planetary motions must be circular. However, single circles could not account for retrograde motion, wherein planets such as Mars appear to move backwards. So Ptolemy proposed that planets are going around smaller circles (epicycles), which are themselves going around a larger circle (the deferent). This allowed him to chart planetary motions with surprising accuracy. Yet scientists today agree that there are no epicycles and that Ptolemy's model of the solar system is mistaken. We may conclude that today's theories, which seem useful and plausible to modern scientists, may also be seriously in error.

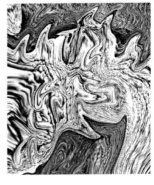

3. Some scientific claims made today are regarded as established facts that cannot be legitimately questioned. What would be a better way of viewing these claims?

Second, when scientific results are held to be certain, the claim usually depends not strictly on science, but on a prior worldview. For example, the statement that the human genome project has traced the complete blueprint for humanity rests on the assumption that we are nothing but material entities, like rocks or minerals. A Christian should be aware that there is a spiritual dimension to humanity that transcends the physical characteristics studied by natural science.

4. Consider this claim: science has proven that there can be no miracles. Where might confidence that miracles are impossible derive from? Does science prove this?

Third, powerful scientific instruments do not necessarily improve life. And even with good intentions, technology leads to unforeseen problems. Radiation can be used to treat cancer but can also produce it. The overuse of antibiotics has produced more virulent strains of bacteria.

5. Are there any deliberately harmful ways science is used today?

What are some other unintended harmful consequences of scientific advances?

Believers sometimes overemphasize the failures of science. Science can be misused, but it can also be a means of serving our neighbor. For example, early scientists like Robert Boyle (1627–91) saw chemistry as a means of providing inexpensive medicines for the poor. Probably the most important advances for public health have been the provision of clean drinking water and the sterilization of medical instruments, both of which depended on scientific discoveries.

6. At its best, what are some of the blessings of science? When God calls us to love our neighbor, how can science provide the physical means to do so?

Both believers and unbelievers tend to suppose that science is a purely human institution. Having an inflated sense of human goodness, unbelievers often exaggerate the blessings of science. Having an understanding of original sin, believers often fixate on the abuses of science. Both can learn from the biblical record.

The Limits of Science

S cience does not threaten Christians. But science that views itself as disconnected from God does threaten Christians and everyone else!

The idea that scientists can find ultimate truth by their own reason denies the true relationship between God and mankind. Frustration will follow when science is viewed as a means of engineering a heaven on earth. We need to remember that the fall into sin has affected all of our abilities, including our reason. Even when our logic is correct, we tend to use it for corrupt goals.

In the late nineteenth century, there was enormous confidence that improvements in the quality of life were guaranteed by scientific innovations in technology. Indeed, this scientific pride was so great that some, following Karl Marx, thought they could devise a scientific method for organizing society.

Then came the First World War, in which the very latest technological innovations were used to kill millions of people in horrific ways. The Soviet Union attempted to use Karl Marx's ideas, leading to a brutal totalitarian regime marked by mass purges and exile to labor camps of millions of "antisocial elements," that is, people who would not conform to the system.

7. Read Genesis 11:1–9. What may the story of the tower of Babel teach us about the limitations of autonomous science? How are the consequences for the people of Babel mirrored by more recent events?

8. Read Psalm 51:3–6. What truth does King David confess about the human condition? How does this show that science alone can never create a heaven on earth?

Autonomous science assumes a utopian result because it denies the fundamental truth that even the most enlightened scientists are infected with original sin, a problem that cannot be solved by pills, surgery, or psychotherapy. The idea of science as salvation proposes that evil is only in the world or in social institutions, and that we can fix all these problems with human ingenuity. But the truth is that evil is within us and is liable to corrupt all human projects.

These prideful abuses of science make some Christians shy away from appreciating the value of science. But there is a legitimate vocation (calling) of scientist. A *vocation* is a station of work that God calls us to, as a means of providing for the needs of others. From the sixth day of creation, we see that God is not a "micromanager." He delegates responsibility to human beings. After God created our first parents, He appointed them as stewards of the rest of creation (Genesis 1:28–30). Likewise, He gave Adam the task of classifying the kinds of animals (Genesis 2:19–20). Even after the fall, human beings are still stewards of their natural environment, although now the task is more difficult (Genesis 3:17–19).

The commission to be "gardeners" of Eden is sometimes called the "cultural mandate." *Culture* can be defined as what humans do to nature to make it suit their purposes. Vocations are means of making cultural products to serve our neighbor. Science provides powerful ways of controlling nature (making cultural products) for the benefit of others. That is why there is a legitimate vocation of scientist.

When scientists or others use science as a means of harming others, they are no longer serving their neighbor. But this shows that they are acting outside of their true vocation, not that there is something wrong with the vocation itself.

9. How would seeing science as a vocation help prevent some of the dreadful abuses of science we mentioned earlier? What good and positive results are or could be achieved today by seeing science as a vocation?

Masks of God

When it comes to salvation, all vocations are equal. They are all equal because they are equally irrelevant! What work could we do to "help" God? As a vocation, science has nothing to do with salvation. God does not *need* our vocations, but our neighbors do.

God sets us free to serve those around us. The sixteenth-century church reformer Martin Luther explained that in this service we are nothing less than "masks of God" (*larvae dei*): we are the visible means through which God provides for others. What is more, there is much that God wants us to do to serve others (Ephesians 2:10).

10. Read Ephesians 2:8–10; Romans 12:4–8; and 1 Corinthians 12:12–26. What do these verses tell us about vocations, including the vocation of scientist? What comfort can they provide when we are unsure of our path in life; for example, if we are wondering whether we can be a faithful disciple of Christ and a scientist?

The fact that God uses us as instruments of His providential care is all the more remarkable because we are still in a fallen state. Even Christians, freely saved by Christ's righteousness, still retain the old Adam and remain sinful. Yet God can work through sinful human beings to provide for others.

Even when scientists have sinful motives of greed or lust for fame, their discoveries may still benefit others. Even though a medical scientist might develop a wonder drug to make himself wealthy and famous, the drug itself may be used to benefit many people. By contrast, the scientist who is a Christian is set free to serve and may develop the drug for a better reason. In gratitude for what Christ has done in saving us, a Christian may gladly and freely serve others as a scientist.

11. Read Genesis 50:15–21 from the story of Joseph. What does this tell us about how God provides? (See especially v. 20.) What comfort can that provide us in our daily lives?

12. How do these events in Joseph's life prefigure the life of Jesus Christ? (See John 11:47–53.) What does that tell us about God's love?

We should be comforted by the fact that our salvation does not depend on how we use our gifts, and also by the fact that there are many different ways God can use us to achieve His ends. We may now be more willing to encourage talented young people to become scientists in service to others. If we feel that science may sometimes be abused, we can encourage more Christians to become scientists so they can be salt and light in the scientific community (Matthew 5:13–16).

In our individualistic age, we tend to think that everything we do is a choice, but vocations are really sent to us by God. Although we can choose whether or not to follow the vocation, and how we will follow it, the calling comes to us through our gifts and circumstances. We do not create it by our own choice.

13. Read 1 Corinthians 7:17–24, especially verses 17 and 20. What do these verses tell us about the nature of vocation? How do they aid Christians who wonder whether or not their work is really "right for them"?

Thanks be to God for the *vocation* of our Lord Jesus Christ. The heavenly Father called Him to create us anew through Baptism in His name. He perfectly fulfilled His calling so that He might atone for the sins we commit in our callings. Through Christ we live and work to the Father's glory and the good of all.

Words to Remember

For we are God's workmanship, created in Christ Jesus to do good works, which God prepared in advance for us to do. (Ephesians 2:10)

17

CHAPTER TWO

Science as Sub-creation

S cience "creates" so many products that some people see scientists as creators in the same sense that God is the Creator. For example, God said, "Let there be light" (Genesis 1:3) and there was light. Scientists have figured out how to generate and direct electricity to create artificial light for when the sun goes down. God said, "Let Us make man" (Genesis 1:26). Now life scientists can use germ-line therapy to prevent mankind's offspring from acquiring a hereditary disease. Others are proposing to make people through cloning.

If humans can be cloned successfully, will scientists be their creators? And if so, does this mean that the clones are made in the image of the scientists and not in God's image? If scientists can manufacture a person, can they own that person? It seems to some that there is less and less room to affirm God as Creator.

14. Read Psalm 104:29–35. How does the psalmist respond to God's creative activity?

Some now claim science has "shown" that even humans are not made in God's image. They argue that the examination of human and animal genomes shows that humans are fundamentally similar to other species. They cite this as proof that humans have simply evolved by the undirected processes of random mutation and natural selection. Thus humans have no special dignity, being made in the image of what modern-day scientists Richard Dawkins and Daniel Dennett call respectively the "blind watchmaker" and "Mother Nature."

But if human beings are not made in the image of God, they are not like God and do not have any special powers. This seems an odd conclusion for some scientists to reach, since the ability to do science is precisely something that distinguishes human beings from all other creatures on earth.

15. Why is it that other creatures, such as chimpanzees, who share so many genes with humans, do not develop theories, design instruments and experiments, make predictions, and offer explanations to make sense of or control the world around them? Read and reflect on Psalm 8:4–9.

Creativity

Creation is an ambiguous word. Before God created the universe, there was no other thing in existence except God Himself. So God created the universe without drawing on any other created thing. He also created human beings in a special way, in His own image (Genesis 1:26–27). This is primary creation. Scientists are not capable of primary creation. When a scientist "creates" something, he or she is harnessing or rearranging forces or materials that already exist. The product is often highly novel, and would not have existed without the scientist's ingenuity, but it was assembled from pre-existing elements. Scientists, therefore, engage in secondary creation. They take the elements of primary creation and rearrange them in various useful ways.

J. R. R. Tolkien (1892–1973), the famous writer of *The Hobbit* and *The Lord of the Rings* trilogy, said that humans are "sub-creators." They are used by God in His continuing providential care of the world to create cultural products that benefit others.

16. Suppose that someone says that a scientist has created electrical current and artificial light. How might you respond to such a claim? What is the person overlooking?

Humans now use their sub-creativity to produce machines that can themselves "create." A cleverly programmed computer can "create" output such as spreadsheets or slideshows. Complex computers at manufacturing facilities can now generate products. As a result, laborers have found themselves replaced by machines. Some even worry that computers will make human labor obsolete.

However, computers have even less creative power than humans. Human creativity involves imagination, foresight, and planning. Humans can develop a blueprint for a complex structure before building it. Human creativity is goal directed and intentional. Computers passively implement human goals. They have no goals of their own. Computers engage in tertiary creation. They are made in the image of humans but not in the image of God. Our being "like God" does not mean we are at the same level as God. In a similar way, the fact that computers can behave like humans does not mean they have the same level of creative capacity as we do.

17. Suppose someone says that an artificially intelligent chess program is a very creative chess player? What is the person overlooking?

Humans are also different from computers in that they have a will. Computers are completely deterministic devices. Given their program and input, they inevitably produce a particular output. Human beings, on the other hand, can make choices and may produce highly individual work. When computers "create," what they create lacks their influence. This is also true of everything humans develop. For example, Albert Einstein had an active will, but his theory of relativity does not.

18. The human will demonstrates incredible creativity, which honors the Lord who made it. How is the human will likewise a disappointment and a dishonor to the Lord? Read Genesis 6:5–6.

What happens when humans interfere in the production of human life? If scientists clone human beings, would the clones lack a personal will and only be made in the image of man? Here it is important to remember that humans who have not been cloned—like you and me—are not the direct creation of God. Today God creates indirectly, working through means such as parents. God creates new human beings through the natural reproduction process, which He established at creation. The fact that human activity is involved does not mean that the offspring are only made in a human image.

Human reproduction unites cells containing information that already existed and that stems from God's creating work. So if scientists clone humans, they may modify what unaided nature would do (secondary creation), but the scientists will not be the source of the original information that specifies the physical and spiritual characteristics of humans. There is every reason to think that a human clone would still be made in the image of God and have a personal will and foresight.

19. What is morally problematic about human cloning? How is the clone being treated? What are the motives for cloning? Is there a legitimate vocation of human cloning?

Humble
before Our Maker

Human beings should never be viewed as manufactured products. A spiritual danger of human cloning is that the scientist falsely sees himself as a god (Genesis 3:5), as a primary creator, and that what the scientist creates is seen as being less than a human being, as simply technology, like a computer. The great German philosopher Immanuel Kant (1724–1804) asserted that we should never treat other human beings as a means to our own ends. As our Creator, God has the right to "use" us in this way. He not only has the right, He also has a good and perfect will in the exercise of that right (Romans 8:28; 12:2). Through our vocations we are means of His creating work.

We are not the Creator. Other human beings are not our creatures. They have dignity equal to our own. For they, like us, are made in God's image.

20. Even without cloning, we are often tempted to treat other human beings as inferior, as means to our ends. What are some examples of this tendency? How should Christians respond when this happens?

Atheists are tempted not only to view scientists as primary creators, but also to hold that these scientists are uncreated beings! This is not because they think scientists are like God, existing from eternity, but because they think scientists are the products of the blind, undirected process of natural selection.

This thinking results in an odd contradiction. At the very same time that a scientist's creative gifts of imagination, foresight, and planning are exalted, it is maintained that the scientist was produced by a process devoid of imagination, foresight, and planning!

21. What problem for the evolutionist's picture of the scientist does this contradiction reveal? Explain and defend your answer.

In his book *Miracles* (1947), C. S. Lewis (1898–1963) refuted the evolutionary naturalist's picture of life. He demonstrated that when we argue logically, we see in advance that a conclusion must follow. For example, if we assume that A=B and that B=C, we can also know that A=C.

What C. S. Lewis pointed out was that logical thought and morality are quite different from natural physical processes. Natural (undirected) processes (1) simply occur, (2) are not trying to get anywhere, and (3) could have been otherwise. In contrast, logical thought specifies (1) what we ought to believe, (2) how we can use it, and—if the argument is valid— (3) what conclusion must follow.

Like logic, the "oughts" of morality do not arise from the facts of natural science. Our access to logical and moral thought reveals a realm that stands over nature and can never be derived from it. But for naturalists, all we can claim is that one event happens to follow another event, and natural events do not have goals. (E.g., the boulder tumbling down the hillside is not trying to reach the valley below.)

In our moral thinking we see that things ought to be done in certain ways. But in the naturalist worldview, all we learn is what is done, without an investigation of whether it should or should not have been done. It is a logical fallacy to argue that because something is the case, therefore it ought to be the case.

Atheists exaggerate human creativity, putting us on the same level as God, but they belittle it, reducing us to machines. A Christian contribution for understanding human creativity is to affirm what Stanley Jaki (b. 1924) calls "the middle road." Scientists are not God. But they are not merely manufactured products or the result of chance. Humans are made in the image of God, so we do have special abilities to imagine, foresee, and plan. These special abilities give scientists a wonderful means of serving others and also the potential to enslave and harm them. Therefore, scientists are no more (or less) important than other human beings. All people in every useful vocation are created in God's image and called to serve Him. Scientists should therefore pursue the "middle road" that accurately reflects the true relationship between all humans and God.

22. What are some practical examples where scientists should be seeking the middle road, but are tempted to go above or below it?

God's Calling

The deification of science is a pathetic attempt to usurp God's vocation and leads some humans to dehumanize their fellows. We are like God in certain respects, but lack His power, wisdom, and knowledge. And since the fall, we lack original righteousness and stand condemned.

But thankfully our salvation does not depend on us being just like God. The central message of Holy Scripture is that works, including scientific works, save no one. The apostle Paul asks, "Where, then, is boasting? It is excluded. On what principle? On that of observing the law? No, but on that of faith. For we maintain that a man is justified by faith apart from observing the law" (Romans 3:27–28). We did not have to attain a certain level of goodness or intellectual enlightenment to receive this gift. Salvation is a free gift of love. "But God demonstrates His own love for us in this: While we were still sinners, Christ died for us" (Romans 5:8).

23. Why is this message a message of hope for a scientist who despairs of finding cures for all the diseases that ravage the world?

The wonderful, free gift of salvation is available to all. Since Christ died to redeem all people, we can see that all people are equally important in God's eyes. From this perspective, we can see how wrong it is to treat others as our inferiors, as experimental subjects, biological resources, or subversives who need "reconditioning" to suit the purposes of the state. For as God loved us, so we are called to love others, unconditionally, regardless of their sins, whether or not we like them or they suit our purposes. Indeed, "We love because He first loved us. If anyone says, 'I love God,' yet hates his brother, he is a liar. For anyone who does not love his brother, whom he has seen, cannot love God, whom he has not seen. And He has given us this command: Whoever loves God must also love his brother" (1 John 4:19–21).

What surpassing love Jesus shows for you, your brothers and sisters, and even His own enemies! While we were still sinners and hostile toward God, Jesus laid down His life for one and all (Romans 5:8–11). Despite your sin, no matter what your calling, Christ loves and treasures you. He displayed this love on the cross. He continues to display this love through the blessings He gives through His church, the creation, and the good works of all.

24. What opportunities do scientists have for displaying the love of God? What are some examples?

Brotherly love cannot, however, be compelled from someone but is a fruit of faith. When we see Jesus as our Savior, we see our own sinful condition accurately and can no longer see others as inferior. Indeed, as C. S. Lewis once said, we are "fellow patients in the same hospital," and if some have an advantage, it is not because they need treatment any the less, but because they know the doctor, Jesus Christ. The "sinners club" includes all of fallen humanity, including the most brilliant scientists. "There is no one righteous, not even one" (Romans 3:10). But God in Jesus Christ has "appeared once for all at the end of the ages to do away with sin by the sacrifice of Himself" (Hebrews 9:26). The payment is complete, requiring nothing further on our part, and is made available to all through faith.

25. How can an accurate picture of our sin and total dependence on Christ transform a scientist who used to see others as inferior?

From this perspective, scientists should no longer see other human beings, or themselves, as insignificant by-products of a natural process that did not have them in mind. Rather, because we all are redeemed by God, the task of the scientist is to use his or her special gifts to reflect the love that God has showered upon us. Scientists who minister to the bodily needs of others have wonderful credibility when they share the Gospel.

Words to Remember

When I consider Your heavens, the work of Your fingers, the moon and the stars, which You have set in place, what is man that You are mindful of him, the son of man that You care for him? You made him a little lower than the heavenly beings and crowned him with glory and honor. You made him ruler over the works of Your hands; You put everything under his feet: all flocks and herds, and the beasts of the field, the birds of the air, and the fish of the sea, all that swim the paths of the seas. (Psalm 8:3–8) ·

CHAPTER THREE

How Theology Gave Birth to Modern Science

Many people have heard and believe that science and Christianity are in an irreconcilable conflict. Andrew Dickson White (1832–1918) made a very influential defense of this thesis in *A History of the Warfare of Science with Theology in Christendom*, published in 1896. White portrays the Christian church as dogmatic and oppressive, clinging to outmoded superstition in the face of experimental evidence. He portrays scientists as enlightened, liberated thinkers who will usher in a new era of peace, prosperity, and tolerance. Many support White's conclusions by arguing that Luther opposed Copernicus's heliocentric model of our planetary system and that the Roman Catholic Church opposed Galileo because of conflicts between science and Scripture.

At the same time, some assume that science does not fit well with orthodox Christianity because of the latter's reliance on supernatural miracles, especially the incarnation (God's becoming man) and the resurrection. Science, it is thought, must investigate the natural world as if God's actions were undetectable. The idea is that science can only investigate natural causes of natural effects, and so divine activity in the world is beyond the concern of science.

26. What other examples might people offer of conflicts between Christianity and scientists?

Some scientists take a view called "methodological naturalism." They proceed in their work as if there were no God at work in nature, but they are free to believe in nature as a matter of faith. Others hold to "philosophical naturalism," according to which nature is all there is. This view denies miracles and the existence of God.

Some argue that scientists are inevitably drawn to philosophical naturalism. Others argue that it is all right for a Christian who is a scientist to be a methodological naturalist. They deny that God may allow both believers and unbelievers to know that a creator is at work in nature.

Theology Yields Science

R ecent work in the history of science thoroughly discredits Andrew Dickson White's "warfare" thesis. Numerous contemporary works show that Christian theology was actually a major impetus to the rise of modern science. As Nancy Pearcey and Charles Thaxton argue in their book *The Soul of Science* (Crossway Books, 1994), there are many non-Christian religions and worldviews that are antithetical to science. For pantheism, the spiritual is entirely within nature, making investigation of the natural world sacrilegious. Polytheism implies that events are governed by independent, capricious, local deities, undermining any basis for believing in uniform natural laws. Stanley Jaki points out in *The Savior of Science* (Wm. B. Eerdmans, 2000) that Christian theology contributed the idea of a transcendent, rational Creator who made humans in His own image.

27. What does *transcendent* mean? How does the fact that God

transcends His creation make scientific study of nature permissible? Read Psalm 139:7–10; 1 Kings 8:22–23, 27; and 1 Kings 4:29–34.

28. Why does the fact that the Christian God is a rational God, who made humans in His own image, give us confidence that good science is something we can actually do?

Modern science did not appear until the late sixteenth century. Someone might ask, "If Christian theology was so congenial to science, why did it take so long for science to develop when the church had already existed for about 1,600 years?" Peter Harrison argues in his book *The Bible, Protestantism and the Rise of Natural Science*, that one main answer is found in medieval Scholasticism. The Scholastics had a tremendous veneration for ancient texts, not merely Scripture, but also the classics of the Greco-Roman world. Aristotle (384–322 B.C.) was viewed as *the* philosopher, and it was standard practice to explain natural events by showing how they fell under the Aristotelian scheme of science.

Scholastic science relied on preconceived metaphysics and supposed it could anticipate nature's operation. But if one thinks one knows what nature must be up to, one is discouraged from actually investigating nature. Why do an experiment if you already know the result?

At the same time, following the allegorical approach to interpretation of the Bible used by some early church fathers, allegory was likewise used to interpret the natural world. Allegory interprets things as symbols. It places emphasis on discovering the higher truth that stands behind an object or an action. For example, allegorists interpreted Jesus' freeing of the doves during the cleansing of the temple (John 2:12–22) to mean that He frees our souls. They concluded this

31

because in ancient symbolism, a dove represented the soul or spirit. Allegorists would focus so completely on the symbolic potential of something that they would fail to consider the thing itself.

For the allegorist, animals were created by God to teach us moral lessons, which were described in various stories called "bestiaries." Insights of ancient writers were held in high regard and the figurative meaning of an animal was not something that could be detected with the naked eye. It was therefore thought more profitable to study the ancient authorities than to make careful observations of animal behavior. As a result, incorrect views were often retained. For example, St. Ambrose suggested that, in Christlike manner, the pelican wounds its breast to feed its starving young. This is touchingly pious but scientifically inaccurate.

29. How is an allegorical approach to the natural world an obstacle to genuine scientific understanding?

The Reformation made a decisive contribution to the emergence of modern science. The reformers realized that allegorical interpretations of the Bible were speculative. For authoritative church doctrine, what matters is the plain, natural meaning of the text. By careful study, Martin Luther realized that the medieval church had obscured the plain scriptural teaching of justification by grace alone because it did not focus on what the Scripture actually said.

The change from an allegorical to a "natural" method of interpreting Scripture was carried over to the natural world. Now what mattered was discerning the patterns that God had literally inscribed in nature. The forefront of modern science included Lutherans, such as Tycho Brahe (1546–1601), Johannes Kepler (1571–1630), and Joachim Rheticus (1514–74). For Kepler, scientists were "priests of the highest God in regard to the book of nature," called to "think God's thoughts after Him." Contrary to the "warfare" theory about science and theology, Luther encouraged Rheticus to explore Copernicus's theory at Wittenberg. And recent scholarship suggests that the Catholic church opposed Galileo because his views conflicted with Aristotelian philosophy and scientific observation, not because he contradicted Scripture.

30. Why is a literal or natural approach so important to science?

The Book
of Nature

E ven after the fall, humans have
the ability to make sense of God's
creation. When the best minds of the
Scholastic era thought they should learn
about creation by reading the ancients,
they were closing their eyes to the book in front of everyone's eyes.
This book of creation is not mute, and we do have the gifts to read
what it says. As the psalmist writes, "The heavens declare the glory
of God; the skies proclaim the work of His hands. Day after day they
pour forth speech; night after night they display knowledge. There
is no speech or language where their voice is not heard. Their voice
goes out into all the earth, their words to the end of the world" (Psalm
19:1–4).

31. What does it tell us about God's creation that it contains
"speech." How does this encourage scientific study?

The Reformation helped human beings use their God-given faculties to discern the clear messages that God Himself had provided,
both in Scripture and His other book, the book of nature. But in order
for a book to be read and its message discerned, one must suppose

that the book has an author. Methodological naturalism pretends that we can read nature on the assumption that the message was inscribed by nature itself. But without God, the blind, undirected processes of nature can only produce an incoherent and meaningless text.

It is important to combat the view quite prevalent today that a Christian who is a scientist should have no problem being a methodological naturalist. Methodological naturalism closes nature to the source of its intelligibility and yields a muted nature, incompatible and quite different from the one described in Scripture.

Some theologians argue that our rational faculties are so damaged by the fall that we can no longer understand God's work in creation without the regeneration of saving faith. They then argue that, because scientific results must be accessible to all scientists, regardless of faith, these results will not include pointers to the divine. But if the consequences of the fall were as severe as this, surely we would be unable to understand this very theological truth! And in any case, this skeptical view does not agree with the scriptural teaching of the natural knowledge of God. "For since the creation of the world God's invisible qualities—His eternal power and divine nature—have been clearly seen, being understood from what has been made, so that men are without excuse" (Romans 1:20). It is clear that this knowledge is available to unbelievers—this is why they are "without excuse"—so it cannot be maintained that it falls outside the realm of scientific knowledge because it can only be discerned through the eyes of faith.

32. Read Romans 1:18–25. What is the real reason some people cannot see God's work in nature?

Not only is it possible to see God's handiwork, but Christians are also called to study God's "other book." Kepler had trained to be a pastor, but felt unable to go into the ministry. His mathematical brilliance suited him to astronomy, but he wondered if it was God-pleasing. The Reformation doctrine of vocation showed Kepler that one could be called to astronomy. And the "priesthood of all believers," together with the idea that nature was a book, showed him that one could be a "priest" in the book of nature, seeing the whole universe as a kind of temple where study would glorify God.

33. How does seeing science as a kind of priesthood encourage both the humility and confidence required to do great science?

Transcendent and Intimate

S cientists are not saved because they view their work in a certain way. The majority of Christians who are sci-entists do follow methodological naturalism because, since the Enlightenment, this is how scientists are trained. In many areas, the approach is successful because scientists are only studying the immediate or proximate causes of things, and not their ultimate explanation. Whether scientists choose to consider God's work in nature or not, it was God's supernatural intervention in our world in the incarnation and resurrection of the Son of God that saved all of us from our sins, including the sin of closing our eyes to God's messages for us. In case there was any doubt that God was the author of the natural text, the author appeared as a character in the story, with a divine and human nature united in the person of Jesus Christ. He lived, died, and rose again in the same history that we all inhabit.

34. What problem does this reveal for religions such as Islam, which maintains that its god is wholly transcendent and would not dirty himself by becoming man?

Viewing science in a biblical way, as a priesthood in the book of nature, does not save anyone. It simply teaches what the vocation of science is really about: reading the inscriptions and traces that God has left behind in creation. But ultimately such priesthood is intended to show ways of serving our neighbors. It does not serve God, and it does not save us.

For salvation, the only priest that matters is Jesus Christ, who was "made like His brothers"—fellow humans—"in every way, in order that He might become a merciful and faithful high priest in service to God, and that He might make atonement for the sins of the people" (Hebrews 2:17). God is not an aloof high priest who is unable to understand the weaknesses and temptations of human beings, including scientists.

Scientists are tempted to claim they know more than they do or to claim that their work has nothing to do with God. They may see their work only as a means to power, fame, and wealth. But there is comfort in Christ, for He shows His complete solidarity with human affliction. "For we do not have a high priest who is unable to sympathize with our weaknesses, but we have one who has been tempted in every way, just as we are—yet was without sin" (Hebrews 4:15). The perfect life that we could not lead has been lived by Christ. The perfect payment that we could not pay has been paid in full by His death on the cross for all our sins.

35. How does the priesthood of science differ from Jesus' priesthood? How does that provide comfort and direction to a scientist who is a Christian?

Christians who are scientists know they do not have to construct meaning. Meaning is out there and is God-given, waiting to be discovered. Einstein said that the most incomprehensible thing about the universe is that it is comprehensible. But this should not surprise Christians. Even after the fall, the universe and the human mind reflect the rational design of the Creator. Although the story went wrong, as C. S. Lewis once said, God provided the "missing passage" that makes sense of it all.

36. Read Colossians 1:16–17. How does the supremacy of Christ give confidence to the scientist who is a Christian?

Words
to Remember

T he God who made the world and everything in it is the Lord of heaven and earth and does not live in temples built by hands. And He is not served by human hands, as if He needed anything, because He Himself gives all men life and breath and everything else. (Acts 17:24–25)

CHAPTER FOUR

Science Serves Our Neighbors

T he stereotype of the "mad scientist" expresses the fear that scientists may be so consumed by their desire to know how things work, and to make things happen, that they lose good judgment and act unethically. Mary  Shelley's story *Frankenstein* (1818) highlights the lack of concern for basic moral values that may arise when human life is viewed merely as an object of experimental investigation. *Frankenstein* is, of course, science fiction.

But today we see scientists engaged in stem cell research, disregarding questions raised about the God-given value of all human life. We hear of scientists paid by tobacco companies to create the false impression that there are no significant health risks associated with smoking. We see pharmaceutical scientists developing more and more drugs that are aggressively marketed. Some of this marketing tempts people who do not need the drugs to demand that their doctor (another scientist) prescribe them. Against better judgment, he or she sometimes does just that. All of this makes us wonder whether science can really be a moral enterprise.

37. As a group, list other moral dilemmas raised by scientific activities. Which ones concern you most?

According to some critics, much of science is inherently immoral because it attempts to play God. They question whether science is really about helping others or about glorifying the powers of the scientist and providing products we would really be better off without, but find almost impossible to resist. Others see science as simply amoral, as a powerful instrument that can be used for good or evil. Scientists themselves sometimes excuse work that they know will be used unethically, saying they are only "concerned with the truth" and how that truth is used is someone else's business. The idea that science is a vocation that falls under God's Law is virtually absent. The idea that scientists are citizens and brothers and sisters of all other human beings is not considered often enough.

Science and Morality

As we have seen in Chapter 1, humans have been given a "cultural mandate" to subdue the earth. One of the ways they can do this is through the vocation of science. Also we have noted that the world is no longer perfect. It is a fallen world afflicted with disease, discomfort, drudgery, and poverty. Many of the early scientists saw their work as a means of easing the consequences of the fall. For example, Robert Boyle became interested in chemistry partly because he hoped to make inexpensive remedies for the many ailments afflicting the poor. To scientists such as Boyle, science was conceived within a moral context, as necessarily serving the needs of fallen humanity. It was not directed at harm or selfish gain, nor was it viewed merely as an instrument to be used in good ways and bad.

38. How does viewing science as a vocation restore its moral dimension? What can we say to those modern scientists who say they are "just doing their job" and need not concern themselves with how their results are used?

We need to be careful. All vocations are under God's Law. Some ways of finding cures or laborsaving devices may indeed be immoral. Furthermore, the unnecessary or excessive use of some of these items may reflect poor stewardship and do more harm than good. Efficient, reliable transportation is a great boon of scientific technology. Yet there are also many inefficient vehicles that drain resources and produce unnecessary pollution. While humans are given dominion over creation, it is a dominion of stewardship, not a license for wasteful greed and practices that poison the air, earth, and water.

39. How does the vocation of scientist provide an ethic for environmental care? How is this ethic markedly different from the extremes of "nature worship" or unrestrained exploitation and development? In this regard, how is it helpful to see the scientist as a kind of "gardener"?

Scientists are not called to be gods, usurping God's lordship over life and death. It is important to consider the implications of Jaki's "middle road" for scientific ethics. When scientists treat human life as a disposable, experimental item, they act outside of their vocation. For example, the Nazi scientists engaged in some hideously dehumanizing experiments. In one, they placed prisoners in a refrigerated room and lowered the temperature progressively to find out at what point a human being would die of hypothermia. Another horrific idea is cloning human beings to provide "spare parts" for other human beings. Such experiments violate Kant's requirement that we should never treat human beings as simply a means to other ends. Although scientists are called to mitigate the consequences of the fall, not all ways of doing this are morally acceptable.

40. What are some other ways in which scientists may be tempted to act outside of their vocation in their treatment of human beings?

Many scientists pursue highly ethical research from which many human beings benefit. For example, geneticists have discovered the specific causes of such hereditary diseases as cystic fibrosis and Tay-Sachs disease. Modern germ-line therapy can do nothing to stop original sin. But it can prevent offspring from suffering some of the temporal consequences of sin.

41. What are some of the triumphs of ethical science? How have these made life better for countless people while using only ethical means to obtain the results?

One Calling among Many

The vocation of science does provide more power to human beings than many other vocations. But we must remember Lord Acton's warning that all power corrupts. We need to be aware that science should be constrained by strict guidelines. Since the content of science is the operation of the natural world, and this is a world of "what is," not "what ought to be the case," scientific theories and results cannot themselves tell us how scientists ought to behave. In other words, science has nothing to do with how science is used. But the scientist is an office holder, and all offices are bound by the Law of God. This is true not only for the believer who accepts the validity of God's Law, but also for the unbeliever who does not.

Fundamentally, scientists are no more important than anyone else. They may serve as our intellectual "eyes" when attempting to peer into the secret workings of nature, and they may be the ones who direct the "hand" of those who manufacture and use scientific technology, but "the eye cannot say to the hand, 'I don't need you!'" Scientists may be the intellectual heads of modern society while others are called to walk along paths shaped by science, but "the head cannot say to the feet, 'I don't need you!'" (1 Corinthians 12:21).

42. Read all of 1 Corinthians 12:14–26 in light of the vocation of scientists and other vocations. How can it be argued that scientists are just as dependent on other vocations as other vocations are dependent on scientists?

Fundamentally, we need to see that scientists are not a secular priesthood set apart from others. Scientists are members of the community and are not granted superhuman privileges. The doctrine of vocation helps us by pointing out that vocations are *reciprocal*. For example, as there is a vocation of parent, so there is a vocation of child. As there is a vocation of scientist, so there are various vocations that thrive by the use of scientific products and generate profit. Agricultural scientists develop hardier crops and various pesticides, but they are not superior to the farmers who use their products to grow corn. In fact, the agricultural scientists work with farmers, bakers, truck drivers, retailers, and marketing advisors to bring us our daily bread. Instead of seeing vocations as competing for prestige and preeminence, we can see them cooperating to fulfill God's providential plan.

43. Why do you think some people view scientists as "set apart" from the rest of the community? What can be done to combat this impression?

In any vocation, there is a temptation to see the work as an end in itself. In *The Great Divorce* (1945), C. S. Lewis describes a painter who began his career trying to capture glimpses of heaven, but then became interested in the paint and the artistic process for its own sake. Likewise scientists can be so wrapped up in the machinery of their work that they lose sight of any God-pleasing goal.

Some years ago scientists developed a bovine growth hormone

that increases the milk yield of dairy cows. Not only were there (perhaps unfounded) concerns about the safety of the milk, but also the product seemed curiously unhelpful in a time of milk surpluses! To see science as something to be done for its own sake falls short of seeing it as a wonderful gift for enhancing our ability to help others.

44. Do scientists sometimes do poorly motivated work? What are examples? How can their work be refocused?

United in Christ

Where scientists have acted outside their office, harming others or despoiling God's creation, they need to know that God's forgiveness is for all people. Where scientists have elevated science above God's moral law, the Word gives sight to the blind so that they understand where they truly stand in God's creation and in society. Intellectual sight is not the same as spiritual sight. This is because "the man without the Spirit does not accept the things that come from the Spirit of God, for they are foolishness to him" (1 Corinthians 2:14). And spiritual insight is never received through our sinful human wisdom, but only through Christ's wisdom. "Has not God made foolish the wisdom of the world? For since in the wisdom of God the world through its wisdom did not know Him, God was pleased through the foolishness of what was preached to save those who believe" (1 Corinthians 1:20–21).

Christ is so much more than a wise man or a moral compass. He is for us wisdom from God—that is our righteousness, holiness, and redemption. By His death for our sins He has overcome death. Through His rising to life, He gives us new life, hope, and genuine unity, an eternal bond of love and grace with our Maker.

45. What important spiritual truths are being overlooked when "enlightened" secular scientists claim they alone can discern how best to proceed in science?

Not only does the Gospel bring spiritual sight, it also brings spiritual gifts that enable us to have a proper concern for one another. Scientists transformed by the Gospel cannot view themselves as cut off from other humans, but must see themselves as part of a united body in which they play one role among many that have equal dignity, even though they differ in worldly status. For "God has combined the members of the body and has given greater honor to the parts that lacked it, so that there should be no division in the body, but that its parts should have equal concern for each other" (1 Corinthians 12:24–25). As a result of this unity there is a sense of appreciation and compassionate concern for others. United by Christ, we are not competitors, jockeying for advancement in the world's eyes. We don't live to "get ahead" by elevating ourselves and putting others down. We are "fellow passengers" invested in a common project, as Stephen Carter points out in his book *Civility* (Basic Books, 1998).

It is because of this common project that there can be no justification for using another being for the benefit of only some members of the community. For in the community created by the Gospel, "if one part suffers, every part suffers with it" (1 Corinthians 12:26a). Further, great scientific achievements are not a reason to create an elitist separation of scientists but are beneficial to the whole: "if one part is honored, every part rejoices with it" (1 Corinthians 12:26b). For all, including bright scientists, are called to humility. "Live in harmony with one another. Do not be proud, but be willing to associate with people of low position" (Romans 12:16).

What creates the unity, though, is ultimately not us, but Christ, for "in Him the whole building is joined together and rises to become a holy temple in the Lord" (Ephesians 2:21). And the building is not made by sinful human hands, but by Christ in whom we are "being built together to become a dwelling in which God lives by His Spirit" (Ephesians 2:22).

46. How is the Law alone ultimately unable to guide scientific work? How would faith that comes from the Gospel build up the community of scientists and others?

Words
to Remember

Y ou, my brothers, were called to be free. But do not use your freedom to indulge the sinful nature; rather, serve one another in love. (Galatians 5:13)

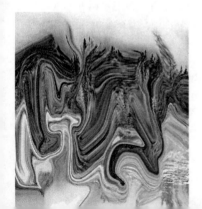

CHAPTER FIVE

Science, Beauty, and God's Handiwork

M any materialists believe that beauty is an accident. These materialists can be called *reductionists.* For them, blind, inarticulate matter is more fundamental than any of the apparent "wonders" it has generated. They believe that the ultimate reality is undirected and random. What lies behind so-called eternal truths of order and rationality is chaos. What lies behind so-called goodness and love is a reality devoid of value or concern. Beauty is a mirage, an arbitrary preference. In place of the true, the good, and the beautiful, these reductionists see the unstable, the indifferent, and the illusory. Behind meaning itself is unmeaning. To use Daniel Dennett's phrase, natural selection is the "unmeant meaner." In other words, natural selection has produced people who believe life has meaning. This is not because life really has meaning, but because such belief helps people survive in a truly meaningless world.

47. Reflect on the implications of the reductionists' beliefs. How might these beliefs affect the scientific discipline?

A second idea of reductionists is that they have reached their stark conclusions simply by examining the facts and applying the scientific method. The claim is that, unlike religious believers, materialist scientists have no biases that color their interpretation.

Francis Bacon once claimed that the way to do science was to eliminate what he called "idols of the mind," various prejudices that attempt to anticipate how the world must be and which therefore distort the data to fit preconceived ideas. The reductionist believes that religious believers are saddled with idols of the mind that predispose religious people to find meaning and purpose, the true, the good, and the beautiful where there is none. By contrast, reductionists believe themselves to be, of all people, the least prone to illusions and idols of the mind. So they believe that they alone courageously assert the naked truth. The idea that no scientist can avoid presuppositions is downplayed. The idea that all scientists, including unbelievers, are committed by their office to meaning, truth, beauty, and goodness is ignored.

48. Briefly set aside personal notions about meaning, truth, beauty, and goodness. Describe what life might look like.

Beauty in Science

The idea that matter is most fundamental is not scientific at all. It is a philosophical, indeed a religious, idea. Looking at the apparent design in the natural world, some people assume there is no God and conclude that the design is only apparent. Looking at the same world and believing in God, others see the apparent design as evidence of a designer. In his book *Miracles*, Lewis makes a similar point about people's interpretations of the marvelous. If we are committed to denying God, then no matter what the evidence, and even if we cannot explain the marvelous event by any known law of nature, we will say that there must be some unknown natural explanation. Looking at the same event, someone who believes in God is open to the possibility that God intervened in nature to produce the event.

49. If a reductionist saw someone who was judged to be dead now living, how might he or she respond?

Reductionists do not reach their conclusions because that is where the facts inexorably lead. They assume that nothing other than a reductionist explanation—one that reduces an apparently meaningful feature to an inherently meaningless one—could be a legitimate scientific explanation, and they interpret the data accordingly. The reductionist view is not a conclusion of scientific study but an assumption that some people make before they start science. The idea that believing in God is a bias, while believing in no God is unbiased, is simply a biased definition of biases! There is no neutral ground here, but only competing biases. A fair approach would be to ask which biases are most fruitful and explanatory.

50. Does believing that one is studying God's handiwork lead to more success in science (the position of Johannes Kepler and Isaac Newton)? Or does believing that one is studying nature's apparent handiwork (the position of reductionists) lead to more success?

51. Philosopher Alvin Plantinga (b. 1932) has raised the worry that if reductionism is true, then it undermines the idea that scientific practice is rational and reliable. If reductionists are right about the design in nature being an illusion, how much confidence can we have in reduction scientists' design of theories and experiments?

Reductionists are naïve to suppose that the ideas of truth, beauty, and goodness can simply be debunked. Reductionists claim to have found the harrowing truth about an indifferent universe, so they are committed to the idea of truth. They think that some ways of doing science are better than others, so they are committed to at least some sort of goodness. And in practice, they prefer scientific theories that are simple, elegant, and coherent over a potentially infinite set of alternative theories that are complex, inelegant, or incoherent. So they are committed to beauty not merely because they like it, but because they see it as a guide to reality. The Nobel Prize–winning atheist physicist Steven Weinberg (b. 1933) admits this in his book *Dreams of a Final Theory* (Vintage Books, 1994). He writes that scientists expect to find "beautiful answers" when they study truly fundamental problems. He notes that the beauty in present theories points toward the beauty of the final theory and that a final theory would not be accepted "unless it were beautiful" (p. 165).

52. If beauty is a guide to truth, how does this undermine reductionism? How can Christians suggest a different explanation of the role of beauty in science?

Truth, Goodness, and Beauty

When reductionists belittle the true, the good, and the beautiful they reveal their lack of faith in the source of these qualities. Jesus says, "I am the way and the truth and the life" (John 14:6). Truth is real, objective, and personal, not an appearance subjectively generated by impersonal matter. The unbelieving picture of truth as disconnected from God is in fact a deception, a denial of the natural knowledge of God implanted in all human beings.

Paul writes that "the wrath of God is being revealed from heaven against all the godlessness and wickedness of men who suppress the truth by their wickedness, since what may be known about God is plain to them, because God has made it plain to them" (Romans 1:18–19). Likewise, God's objective goodness is revealed to all people because "the requirements of the law are written on their hearts" (Romans 2:15). And God has the beauty of a perfect love, reflected in the "beautiful" feet of "those who bring good news"—the messengers of the Gospel (Isaiah 52:7). We also see the beauty of creation: in comparison to "the lilies of the field," "not even Solomon in all his splendor" was as beautifully dressed (Matthew 6:28, 29). Since scientists are concerned with objective truth, they should be concerned with the objective truth, goodness, and beauty that emanate from God's nature.

53. Why is it important for Christians who are scientists to defend the ideas of truth, goodness, and beauty in their work?

Focusing on "higher things" is also good for us, inspiring us to seek truth and meaning and thereby to accomplish good things: "whatever is true, whatever is noble, whatever is right, whatever is pure, whatever is lovely, whatever is admirable—if anything is excellent or praiseworthy—think about such things" (Philippians 4:8). Johannes Kepler believed that our universe was the product of a "divine geometer," and was therefore inspired to find mathematically beautiful laws to explain the planetary orbits. If Kepler had thought that the universe was fundamentally chaotic and planetary motion ugly and irrational, he would not have expected or sought such laws. Believing that life is ugly is self-fulfilling, and leads to negative, nihilistic attitudes and lifestyles. Believing life is beautiful is also self-fulfilling, but leads to brilliant discoveries that reveal truth and help others.

54. A cliché has it that "attitude is everything." While this may overstate the case, how can an attitude oriented to truth, beauty, and goodness encourage scientists to find valuable and useful results?

Ultimately, beauty is not in the eye of the beholder. Looking ahead to the crucifixion, Isaiah wrote of the suffering servant, Jesus Christ, that many would be "appalled at Him—His appearance was so disfigured beyond that of any man and His form marred beyond human likeness" (Isaiah 52:14). From a human point of view, Jesus on the cross "had no beauty or majesty to attract us to Him, nothing in His appearance that we should desire Him" (Isaiah 53:2). Reductionists are right that appearances can be deceiving. But here it is not ugliness that lies behind apparent beauty. Rather, the apparent ugliness of Jesus derives from His bearing our afflictions. The "ugliness" of Jesus is the ugliness of our own sin, which a beautiful Savior took on Himself. For "He was pierced for our transgressions, He was crushed for our iniquities" (Isaiah 53:5).

55. How can Christians, including Christians who are scientists, make the case that beauty may be hidden behind ugly appearances? What are some examples?

Beautiful Savior

A world disconnected from God is a horrible world. Sin not only corrupts the natural world around us but also human faculties of perception and judgment. We do not by nature rightly appreciate the true, the good, and the beautiful, even though we know it is there. However, Scripture tells how Jesus brought sight to the blind and light to a world darkened by sin (Isaiah 9:2). Christ saves us and restores the ability to see the truth, goodness, and beauty of God and His world. It is because of Jesus' taking the ugliness of sin on Himself that we are given the righteousness of God. And because we are reconnected with Him, we can see something of the divine reality that we will one day see perfectly: "Now I know in part; then I shall know fully, even as I am fully known" (1 Corinthians 13:12). Even though we see "a poor reflection as in a mirror," what we see reflects God's glory, His eternal truth, His perfect goodness, and the matchless beauty of His holiness.

56. How does the biblical picture both discourage the arrogant idea that scientists can know everything about the world and yet encourage the idea that scientists can glimpse objective truth?

The Gospel reorients us so that we see the beauty of God's love at work even through the ugliness of sin. In the crucifixion, "the punishment that brought us peace was upon Him, and by His wounds we are healed" (Isaiah 53:5). It is enormously comforting to see that the beauty that matters is God's, not ours, and that any beauty we have is only a reflection of His glory.

Scientists do not need to be motivated by vanity, seeking praises among people for their brilliant discoveries. Rather, they can search in all humility for what is already beautiful and praiseworthy in God's creation. Then they are set free to say "To God alone be the glory." Just as this attitude guided the master musician J. S. Bach to produce beautiful music, so it can inspire scientists to discover beautiful truths about the world we live in. There is a readiness to be surprised, a childlike wonder that can marvel in God's majesty. The paradox is that pursuing one's own greatness leads to falsification of reality, but humbling oneself to God's greatness brings one closer to the truth.

57. How does the Gospel restore a sense of wonder in a Christian who is a scientist? Why does this sense, this openness to truth, goodness, and beauty lead to scientific success?

Christians who are scientists see beauty not only in creation but also in their neighbors. In gratitude for their beautiful Savior, such scientists want to help others. And in those others they can now see

Christ. They know that whatever they do for "one of the least of these brothers of" Christ is done for Christ Himself (Matthew 25:37–40). To see beyond appearances that all people are beautiful as redeemed by Christ restores a sense of human value. Though sin makes us ugly, it is exchanged for the beautiful, white robe of Christ's righteousness. When God the Father looks at us, He does not see the stains and disfigurement of sin, but the perfect, beautiful righteousness of His Son. From this perspective, it is impossible to view another human being as a freak of nature, as a misfit with illusions of truth, beauty, and goodness that do not fit reality.

58. If more scientists saw the beauty of other human beings as redeemed by Christ, what practical effect could this have on how these scientists do their work?

Words
to Remember

Once you were alienated from God and were enemies in your minds because of your evil behavior. But now He has reconciled you by Christ's physical body through death to present you holy in His sight, without blemish and free from accusation. (Colossians 1:21–22)

Defending the Faith with Science

S ome people think that modern science has disproved the Christian faith. Others allow that faith can continue as a sort of private piety affecting one's moral outlook on life but deny that the truth claims of Christianity have any public, objective validity. In both cases, it is claimed that one cannot be a serious, Bible-believing Christian and also a scientist. The main argument for this view rests on the assumption that modern science has succeeded in showing that the material world is all that can really be known. One can choose to believe in something more if one likes, but this is a private preference that can never be backed up by objective scientific evidence.

Behind this outlook is a post-Enlightenment perspective on what counts as science. As Mark Noll documents in his book *The Scandal of the Evangelical Mind* (Wm. B. Eerdmans, 1994), during the later Enlightenment, universities in both Europe and America underwent secularization. Famous schools such as Brown, Harvard, and Yale began with clergy as presidents and regents. They emphasized character formation and Christian theology as an overarching frame of meaning for the curriculum. Then there was a major change to an industrialist model, with businessmen running the colleges and a pragmatic orientation to providing "vocational training" (alas, not in the theological sense). When the paradigm of the German research university reached America, theology was displaced by modern, secular science as the final standard of truth.

59. How did events in Germany during the first half of the twen-

tieth century illustrate weaknesses of the modern, secularist approach to education and life?

Secular science views nature as an autonomous machine, which has no need for God to sustain its operation. This assumes that rigorous scientific investigation of the material world will look to one state of the natural "machine" to explain another state. In other words, the spiritual state of things would never be considered. In consequence, secular scientists equate empirical science (science based on observation) with materialistic science (science that can only infer material causes).

Providence

What is most remarkable about the recent view of science is that it was not held by the founders of modern science. As we saw in Chapter 3, it was ideas from Christian theology that gave birth to modern science. Great scientists such as Kepler and Newton believed in laws of nature because they believed in providence, that God governed His creation by rational means. Kepler never saw his scientific work as disconnected from God's governance. Indeed, as Peter Barker and Bernard Goldstein have argued, Kepler "believed that he had discovered the part of God's providential plan that embodied the pattern of the cosmos, and the divine laws by which God regulated its moving parts" ("Theological Foundations of Kepler's Astronomy," *Osiris 16* [(2001)]: 88–113, p. 113). On this view, laws of nature are not the autonomous principles of a self-sufficient machine, but God's means of governing and sustaining His creation. Newton held a similar view, maintaining that his laws of motion only showed how things moved but not the ultimate source of motion, which was left to God.

60. Today's secular understanding of science cannot really justify its assumption that these are "laws of nature." How would this fundamentally challenge the notions of secular scientists?

It is also false that modern scientists are necessarily driven to compromise their faith. One of the greatest experimental scientists to date was Michael Faraday (1791–1867), director of the Royal Institution in London. Faraday discovered benzene and electromagnetic induction, invented the generator, and was the main architect of the classical field theory of electromagnetism. He also had a robust, orthodox Christian faith. On his deathbed, when asked what new "speculations" he had, he replied: "Speculations, man, I have none! I have certainties. I thank God that I don't rest my dying head upon speculations for 'I know whom I have believed and am persuaded that he is able to keep that which I have committed unto him against that day' [2 Timothy 1:12]." Other great scientists who were committed Christians include James Clerk Maxwell (1831–79), who gave the mathematical interpretation of Faraday's concept of electromagnetic field, now known as "Maxwell's equations"; Sir Joseph John (J. J.) Thomson (1856–1940), discoverer of the electron; and Carolus Linnaeus (1707–78), the father of taxonomy. Francis Collins, current director of the National Institutes of Health Human Genome Project, was an unbeliever who was led by some kind people to read C. S. Lewis and the Bible. He is now an evangelical Christian.

61. Many great scientists, including some atheists, have admitted that science by itself is not enough to make sense of life. How does Christianity provide meaning and orientation to life that science alone cannot provide?

The fact that great scientists can be Christians does not show that their worldview makes sense. Can one do science without assuming materialism?

Phillip Johnson, a Berkeley law professor, has proposed a "wedge" that can be driven between empirical science and materialistic science. Johnson argues that it is a mistake to equate these two models of science, because a scientist can do rigorous empirical investigation without assuming that only material causes are operative and detectable. He explains that it is possible for science to discover a complex phenomenon that unaided nature would not likely produce. For example, if we see that biological information is too complex and tightly specified to have arisen by chance or by any natural law, we may infer a supernatural mind as the cause.

62. Discuss what kind of evidence might convince people that an intelligent agent had intervened in the course of nature. What would convince us that the agent was supernatural and not merely natural?

Logic in Creation

When secular science investigates nature as if nature is disconnected from its Creator, it embarks on the building of a modern Babel, and its thinking becomes "futile" (Romans 1:21). Science as we know it is possible only because the created world and human beings are rational. We should ask what explains the assumption of rationality that must be made before science can begin. Scripture provides an answer: "In the beginning was the Word, and the Word was with God, and the Word was God . . . Through Him all things were made; without Him nothing was made that has been made" (John 1:1–3). Here "Word" is a translation of the Greek word *logos*, which can mean both the Son of God and also a principle of rational order (hence the word *logic*). The apostle Paul states that by Christ "all things were created: things in heaven and on earth, visible and invisible, whether thrones or powers or rulers or authorities; all things were created by Him and for Him. He is before all things, and in Him all things hold together" (Colossians 1:16–17). Christ is the "reason" involved in the creation of the world and human beings, including their reason.

63. How does the Christian idea of Christ as Logos support modern science? What difficulties can be posed for the non-Christian view of science?

Unbelievers do not accept the authority of Scripture, so unless we can evangelize them first, we can only hope to persuade them of our view through reason. This is the idea of Christian *apologetics*.

Apologetics does not mean apologizing for being a Christian, but derives from the Greek word *apologia*, which means "a reasoned, public defense, appealing to objective evidences," as in a court of law. Some Christians oppose this idea, because they see it as an unscriptural attempt to reason someone into the faith, which is impossible, since faith is the work of the Holy Spirit. However, the true goal of apologetics is not conversion, but the removal of obstacles that allow the unbeliever to dismiss the Christian faith without a serious consideration of it. In this sense, apologetics is actually mandated by Scripture: "Always be prepared to give an answer [defense] to everyone who asks you to give the reason for the hope that you have" (1 Peter 3:15).

64. Sir John Polkinghorne (b. 1930), a noted physicist and Anglican clergyman, is a strong defender of the Christian faith. What is it about science that gives Christians who are scientists an excellent opportunity to do apologetics?

Science can be used to defend the faith in a number of key areas. One can argue like C. S. Lewis *(Miracles)*, Angus Menuge *(Agents under Fire* [Rowman & Littlefield, 2004]), Alvin Plantinga *(Warranted Christian Belief* [Oxford University Press, 2000]), and

Victor Reppert (*C. S. Lewis's Dangerous Idea* [InterVarsity Press, 2003]) that the blind, contingent processes of materialistic science cannot explain the goal-directed necessity of the logical thought employed by scientists themselves. One can argue with William Dembski that there are rigorous tests for empirically detecting design in nature (*The Design Inference* [Cambridge University Press, 1998]). One can appeal to the anthropic "coincidences," according to which the universe is very finely tuned to make life as we know it possible (see Larry Witham's By Design [Encounter Books, 2003]). One can point out, as has Stephen C. Meyer (in *Science and Evidence for Design in the Universe* [Ignatius Press, 2001]), that the information in DNA, which partly specifies how proteins are to be assembled to produce various organs, is like the information in a collection of Shakespeare's sonnets, which nobody supposes arose from undirected causes. Finally, with Michael Behe (*Darwin's Black Box* [Free Press, 1996]) one can call attention to "irreducibly complex" structures in biology, which cannot function if a single part is removed, and so challenge the idea of gradual evolution from simpler precursors.

Sciences such as forensics and archaeology show that we do have empirical methods for detecting design. Forensic pathologists are able to tell whether a death was accidental, the lawful outworking of a medical condition, or the result of an evil plan. Detecting a murder involves eliminating chance (accidental death) or law (natural death) in favor of design. Likewise, archaeologists are trained to discriminate between those pieces of matter that have been altered by human shaping (artifacts) and those that have not. There is no question that scientists can detect human design, and it is only dogmatism that leads some to claim that it must be impossible to detect divine design. Sometimes even theologians claim that divine design would be inscrutable, but not only does this deny the scriptural teaching of the natural knowledge of God, but it also presumes we know that God would not want to communicate with us.

65. According to Acts 17:24–31, why did God create the world, compel preachers to speak, and raise Christ from the dead?

Christ,
Our Righteousness

Apologetics can seem a crushing responsibility to many
Christians. There are so many skeptical questions and lines of
defense—who can master them all? However, we are not all required
to be master apologists. The defense we need is mainly for those
we will meet in our vocation. A farmer has a different approach to
defending the faith than a theoretical physicist, and this is just as well
because their vocations put them in contact with different audiences.
Some vocations provide better opportunities for apologetics than others. If we are stumped by a skeptic, we can recommend someone else
whose vocation is better suited to answering the question. Christians
as scientists, however, are an asset to the body of Christ because their
training equips them to analyze evidence and present logical explanations to defend the Christian faith.

66. How does the doctrine of vocation show that apologetics is a
community matter, not an individual matter? How is that comforting to
someone who feels unable to defend the faith effectively?

When we have relevant knowledge, we are sometimes afraid
to use it. Fortunately, we have a God who enables people to speak
out even when they are not "ready." Think of Moses, who claimed
he could not speak, and the astonishing performance of Peter, an
uneducated fisherman, at Pentecost. In fact, there is comfort for us in
the passage immediately preceding the apologist's mandate. Peter's
first epistle was written to Christians suffering persecution, and while
today (in North America at least) Christians are no longer tortured or
executed, they are sometimes ridiculed for their faith. Peter advises,
"Even if you should suffer for what is right, you are blessed. 'Do not
fear what they fear; do not be frightened' [Isaiah 8:12]. But in your
hearts set apart Christ as Lord" (1 Peter 3:14–15). Peter explains that
even if we suffer, "Christ died for sins once for all, the righteous for

the unrighteous, to bring you to God" (1 Peter 3:18). As a result there is nothing we really need to be afraid of anymore. With our salvation assured, we should not fear the world's rejection, which cannot ultimately harm us. Furthermore, it is a focus on Christ and the Spirit's work that will enable us to speak. Our focus, too, should not be conquering individuals who disagree with us (this may put them off the faith), but in helping our neighbors to see the truth.

67. Read 1 Peter 3:15–16. Why do you think it is important to defend the faith with "gentleness and respect"?

Finally, apologetics is never a substitute for faith. At its best, apologetics shows the existence of a designer, or a source of reason or a first cause. But this does not establish that this being is the God of Christianity.

Suppose someone has moved into an apartment above yours, but you have never met the person. You hear certain sounds and form an impression of what sort of individual this is. But you do not know the individual. You do not have a personal relationship. Then one day the newcomer comes down to introduce himself. You come to know him personally. Apologetics gets at qualities of God by examining the world. But faith is a personal relationship made possible only because God came down to us in the person of Jesus Christ.

68. C. S. Lewis once worried that if he was like Hamlet (character) and God was like Shakespeare (author), Lewis could never know God. How does the uniquely Christian claim of the incarnation solve this problem? See John 14:8–9.

Words to Remember

We demolish arguments and every pretension that sets itself up against the knowledge of God, and we take captive every thought to make it obedient to Christ. (2 Corinthians 10:5)

Leader Notes

This guide is provided as a "safety net," a place to turn for help in answering questions and for enriching discussion. It will not answer every question raised in your class. Please read it, along with the questions, before class. Consult it in class only after exploring the Bible references and discussing what they teach. Please note the different abilities of your class members. Some will easily find the Bible passages listed in this study; others will struggle. To make participation easier, team up members of the class. For example, if a question asks you to look up several passages, assign one passage to one group, the second to another, and so on. Divide the work! Let participants present the answers they discover. Also, have participants turn to the glossary at the back of this book for help with technical terms.

Each topic is divided into four sections:

Focus introduces the topic for discussion.

Science critique summarizes what modern science has discovered about the topic.

Law critique considers the topic in view of God's commands.

Gospel affirmation helps participants understand how God addresses the issues raised by the topic through His Son, Jesus Christ.

CHAPTER ONE

God's Intentions for Science

Objectives

By the power of the Holy Spirit working through God's Word, participants will see that science remains subject to God's intentions for human beings; understand why science is not inherently immoral or amoral, but a vocation (calling) bound by God's Law; and understand that although science saves no one, it is a means God uses to provide for our neighbors' needs.

Opening Worship

Invocation

In the name of the Creator, Redeemer, and Sanctifier. Amen.

Readings from God's Word

God blessed them and said to them, "Be fruitful and increase in number; fill the earth and subdue it. Rule over the fish of the sea and the birds of the air and over every living creature that moves on the ground." Genesis 1:28

Now the LORD God had formed out of the ground all the beasts of the field and all the birds of the air. He brought them to the man

to see what he would name them; and whatever the man called each creature, that was its
name. Genesis 2:19

Opening Prayer:

Lord, You have made us stewards over Your
creation and have given us the rational ability to
pursue science. Help us to avoid the pride that
makes our science more important than You.
Help us to see science as a gift, a way that You
work through us to provide for our neighbors'
needs. Above all, show us that salvation is not
found in science, but only in the precious work
of Your Son, Jesus Christ. Amen.

1. Answers will vary.

2. Education and knowledge of themselves do not undermine
faith. In fact, the Lord encourages us to pursue knowledge. However,
pride that comes with success can undermine faith.

3. Encourage participants to share their thoughts and insights.
A scientific claim that some may question is the theory of evolution.
All theories should be treated as theories, even when they are widely
accepted and respected. For more on evolution, see the appendix on p.
93.

4. Science cannot disprove the existence of miracles or a spiritual aspect to life. Science studies events in nature, which may be open
to both natural and supernatural causes.

Most scientists today assume methodological naturalism, according to which scientists should investigate nature as if God had nothing
to do with it. With this frame of mind, nothing is allowed to count as
scientific evidence for a miracle or spiritual existence.

But this does not show a lack of scientific evidence for miracles
or spiritual beings, providing we allow a more open picture of science
that follows the evidence wherever it leads. On a more open model
of science, one may see that a supernatural explanation is sometimes
more likely than a natural one. Suppose you knew that various jars at
the wedding at Cana (John 2:1–11) had been filled with plain water
and, as they were in plain view, you knew they had not been tampered
with. Then someone drew wine from the jars. Naturally, water does
not turn into wine in such a short period or without the addition of

other materials, including grapes. This would be good evidence that a miracle occurred.

The confidence that miracles or spiritual existence are impossible does not come from science at all. It comes from the view that nature is a closed system. However, for Christians, nature is an open system in which God can intervene. Water may naturally stay water, but the Lord of nature, through the same power He used to create water, can turn water into wine.

5. Answers will vary. Today, tyrannical regimes the world over use science to develop deadly chemical and biological weapons. Even in the West, deadly agents such as anthrax were developed during the Second World War, and now may have fallen into the hands of rogue nations. This requires the development of antidotes and safety procedures, also done by means of science.

Even when a good result is intended, there can be bad consequences. The consumption of fossil fuels for heating and transportation has certainly generated pollution and may be causing "global warming." Mechanization, laborsaving devices, and industrialized fast food—all the products of science—are important factors in increased obesity and a decline in health and fitness, although the role of poor choices must not be ignored. Computerization has granted much convenience, but may be bad for our eyes and wrists, and certainly exposes our data to the dangers of worms, viruses, and identity theft.

6. Some of the most important blessings of science seem quite humble and yet have saved and improved the quality of countless lives. Safe disposal of waste, pasteurization, antiseptics, and the development of vaccines have been wonderful achievements. Compassionate scientists have also developed numerous technologies to assist those with impaired senses and those who cannot walk or use their limbs. And they have even developed partial replacements for body parts that are no longer functioning, such as artificial hips and artificial valves for the heart. Although the Internet is also open to abuse, it has allowed valuable communities to form that are not bound by geographical location or the problems of transportation.

7. Answers may vary. Genesis 11 shows us that human reason is a poor substitute for God. Humans cannot by their own reason or strength reach up to God, because God is righteous, all-knowing, and all-powerful, and we are not. All attempts to use science to create a utopia, a heaven on earth, ultimately fail. When God confused the language at Babel, He revealed the cacophony of conflicting, selfish voices that underlie humanity.

History has repeated itself. The nineteenth century idea of inevitable scientific progress was shattered by two world wars, death camps, and totalitarianism. Each of these horrors used science to dehumanize. This led to skepticism about human reason and our current "postmodern times," where there are many competing world-views and groups but no basis for consensus and peace. In this time of confusion, we must come to our senses and confess our sins to God. For "if we confess our sins, He is faithful and just and will forgive us our sins and purify us from all unrighteousness" (1 John 1:9).

8. Sin is not just a problem out there in an uncooperative world that needs to be fixed by technology. It is within us, in our desires for power, wealth, and control of others, and above all in our desire to be our own gods. The truth is that we are by nature sinful from conception and have no power of our own to change this. We are enemies of God and cannot approach God or become godlike by anything we do, including the exercise of our reason in science. Since we are infected with sin, sin manifests itself in any attempt to create a heaven on earth. Our failure is inevitable, but fortunately we are saved by God's grace and can now have the more realistic goal of doing what we can to serve our neighbors out of love.

9. A vocation is an office instituted by God. All such offices are bound by God's Law and are aimed at curbing sin and providing for our neighbors' needs. Seeing science as a vocation would help us keep science in perspective, as a gift to limit evil and help others, not to increase evil and harm others. Seeing science as a vocation would also help us focus more on what our neighbors need and less on making a profit by producing services they might like but that are really unhelpful.

10. We learn from Ephesians 2:8–9 that vocations have nothing to do with salvation. Vocations are directed at works, and we are saved by grace, not works. But vocations are so important to God that He has created good works for us to do in advance (Ephesians 2:10), so that we may aid our neighbor.

The scientist is revealed as merely one part of the body of Christ, which contains many elements, all of which are needed for the body to function, and all of which contribute something of distinctive value. God calls all people to help right where they are and with the gifts they have, and that includes the scientist. The scientist is no better or worse than any other member of the body of Christ, but plays an important contributory role in a wider project that includes those who supply scientists with their needs and those who benefit from scientific results.

It may not always be easy for a Christian to be a scientist (for example, one might work at a lab that has chosen to fund research one believes is unethical), but Christians who are scientists can place their confidence in Christ and do what they can to help others and witness to their faith, just as all Christians are called to do.

11. Joseph's brothers were used by God to place Joseph where he could save many people, including his own family, from starvation. We all experience failure, and scientists may experience it more than most because of the exacting demands of their profession. However, we must remember that God is in charge and that even when we fail, intellectually or morally, God can work through failures to bring success.

12. The leaders in Jerusalem who demanded the crucifixion of an innocent man, Jesus, were used by God in an action that redeemed all mankind. Thankfully, God's love does not falter as ours does, but His love endures forever.

13. Today we think of everything as a choice, not only food and clothes but even beliefs and lifestyles. This way of thinking seduces us into thinking we have everything under control, that we are in charge. But ultimately, God is in charge. He sends us vocations by the gifts He equips us with, the circumstances we find ourselves in, and the neighbors who live beside us. Those people need help, and if we can help them, that is our calling. It may mean crucifying some of our ambitions and desires (vocations are crosses), but as the old self is killed, a new self will appear in Christ, and we are rewarded with a sense of satisfaction in a job well done. We may be tired and overworked, but there is a legitimate sense of achievement in faithful ser-vice to others.

CHAPTER TWO

Science as Sub-creation

Objectives

By the power of the Holy Spirit working through God's Word, participants will understand the different levels of "creation," understand why scientists are not gods, and see that being made in the image of God provides gifts and encouragement for scientific work.

Opening Worship

Invocation

In the name of God the Father, the Son, His perfect image, and the Holy Spirit. Amen.

Readings from God's Word

Then God said, "Let Us make man in Our image, in Our likeness, and let them rule over the fish of the sea and the birds of the air, over the livestock, over all the earth, and over all the creatures that move along the ground." So God created man in His own image, in the image of God He created him; male and female He created them. Genesis 1:26–27

He is the image of the invisible God, the first-born over all creation. For by Him all things were created: things in heaven and on earth, visible and invisible, whether thrones or powers or rulers or authorities; all things were created by Him and for Him. He is before all things, and in Him all things hold together. Colossians 1:15–17

Opening Prayer

Lord God, Father, Son, and Holy Spirit, we worship You alone as God. Help us to see that scientists can never supplant Your roles as Creator and Redeemer. Because we are made in Your image, equip us to serve others. Amen.

14. The psalm as a whole reveals the psalmist's interest in the natural world. Verses 29–35 reveal his sense of awe and worship.

15. Answers may vary. God created humans to have charge of the creation. This distinguishes humans from all other creatures.

16. Although scientists can make light where there was none, what they have done is set up an electrical current and a conductor using existing materials. Electricity consists of electrons, which had already existed. The electric cord contains copper and is coated in plastic synthesized from oil, which had already existed. The glass, tungsten filament, and thread of the bulb were likewise derived from pre-existing sources. Not only that, but if there had been no natural light of the sun to begin with, such scientific work would have been very difficult to do! Only God creates the original resources. Scientists recombine them in clever ways to produce new technologies. In a sense, we always plagiarize from the original author, God.

17. Some chess programs do seem to be very smart, because they appear to learn from their previous games and gradually increase their play level. However, these programs contain two sets of rules; rules that currently guide their behavior and higher-level rules used to modify the weights of the lower-level rules in response to success or failure. If a lower-level rule leads to a win, it is given a higher preference and so is more likely to be used in the future; if it leads to a loss, it is given a lower preference and is less likely to be used.

All of these rules were developed by the programmer, not the programs. More important, it is only the programmer who has the goal of producing a successful program. The program is not trying to win, it is not glad when it does or sad when it does not. People, unlike programs, are agents who act for personal reasons because of something they want to do. Computers cannot act in these ways, though science fiction makes much of the possibility that computers may someday become sentient.

18. Because of the fall into sin, the human will and creativity are thoroughly corrupt and dishonor their Lord.

19. Human cloning is morally problematic because it treats the clone as a product manufactured for the purposes of the person who requests cloning. It is true that natural reproduction also produces people who did not ask to be born, but they are not produced in accordance with a preconceived template solely to serve the whims of the person who makes them or who asked for them to be made.

Motives for cloning are often corrupt as well as illogical. For example, some people would like to replace a son or daughter who died young. But even though a clone would be genetically identical, it would not be the same person. And if it is impossible to recreate the same person, why not "replace" the son or daughter with another child conceived naturally by the parents of the lost child or with an adopted child who needs loving and nurturing parents? With cloning there is a disturbing desire to be in control, to see the child as a means to some end of ours and not as another human being and a gift from God who is called to serve His purposes. To the extent that cloning attempts to exploit a clone, it fails to meet a basic standard or morality taught by our Lord, "Do to others what you would have them do to you" (Matthew 7:12).

Since such exploitation violates God's Law and all vocations are bound by God's Law, there is no such vocation as the vocation of human cloning.

20. Answers will vary. The most obvious example of treating others as a means to our own ends is slavery. Britain, the United States, and many other nations throughout history have found it convenient to claim that other people were inferior, or even less than human, existing to provide a higher standard of living for the beneficiaries. There are disturbing cases of parents who attempt to fulfill their own ambitions vicariously through their children, pressuring them into activities that may not suit them. Among the more ghastly, in my opinion, are efforts to make young girls into "super models."

In a scientific context, fetal stem cell research is premised on the idea that the fetus is not a full human being, but a disposable biological resource that can be used to find cures for other human beings.

Christians should oppose any and every attempt to treat other human beings as inferiors, since all people have the same worth before God.

21. The basic problem for the evolutionist's account is that it undermines confidence that the scientist's faculties are reliable. If we are the product of blind, undirected causes, then the natural conclusion is that we are lacking in foresight and direction. And yet scientists themselves plan experiments and make predictions, activities that require considerable foresight and intentionally directed action. As C. S. Lewis repeatedly pointed out, it is a bad idea to try to use reason to discredit reason: either the attempt fails, or, if it "succeeds," it undermines any basis for saying it did succeed! Evolutionists cannot hope to convince us by argument that their theory is true if their theory implies that argument is not to be trusted.

22. Answers will vary. In the case of genetic engineering, there is much merit in germ-line therapy to prevent a child from receiving an otherwise inherited disease. This approach respects both parent and child and merely attempts to use a sophisticated version of preventive care. Some Christians might oppose this, but scientists would fall short of what they can legitimately accomplish by neglecting this approach. On the other hand, other scientists are tempted to abuse their power to develop enhancements and so-called "designer babies." This is sinful because some people are selecting this design for their own purposes and therefore treat the designer baby as an inferior. They do not see the child as a gift of God, but as a made-to-order product.

23. Salvation is by grace, and we are not called to perfect this world by our works. Such perfection is found only in heaven, and for now we are called to do what we can to serve and witness to our neighbors. Dying of disease may be horrible, but it may also be an escape from this vale of tears. Our hope is not in making this earth a heaven but in the One who draws us and others to His heaven.

24. Scientists can show the love of God by focusing on technologies that respect the full humanity of those who are helped. A good example is the sophisticated adaptation of computers so that they can be used by blind and paralyzed people, and speech synthesizers for those who otherwise cannot speak. At their best, scientists provide the means to "Speak up for those who cannot speak for themselves" (Proverbs 31:8), and thereby show how God spoke up for us by sending Christ to die on our behalf, and to serve as our advocate before God the Father when we had no power to defend ourselves.

25. Seeing everyone as a sinner levels the playing field. If we are "fellow patients in the same hospital," none of us has an inherent advantage over anyone else. Our hope is only in the doctor, Jesus Christ, and as He sets scientists free from bondage to sin, they will, in gratitude, be motivated to do what they can to help their fellow patients along life's way.

CHAPTER THREE

How Theology Gave Birth to Modern Science

Objectives

By the power of the Holy Spirit working through God's Word, participants will see that Christianity and science need not conflict, learn how Christian theology gave birth to modern science, and see the importance of the natural knowledge of God in resisting methodological naturalism.

Opening Worship

Invocation

In the name of the Father, the Son, and the Holy Spirit. Amen.

Readings from God's Word

For since the creation of the world God's invisible qualities—His eternal power and divine nature—have been clearly seen, being understood from what has been made, so that men are without excuse. Romans 1:20

For this reason He had to be made like His brothers in every way, in order that He might become a merciful and faithful high priest in service to God, and that He might make atonement for the sins of the people. Hebrews 2:17

Opening Prayer

Lord, heavenly Father, You have been pleased to provide a priesthood of all believers. Help us to understand that particular priesthood in the book of nature that belongs to scientists. Draw all of us to the higher priesthood of Your Son, who died once and for all for the remission of sins. Amen.

26. Answers will vary. Encourage participants to provide examples from their personal experience or reading.

27. *Transcendent* means "above and beyond" or "not contained." It is to be contrasted with *immanent,* which means "dwelling within." These are both qualities of God, as the quotations from David and Solomon show. The fact that God is transcendent means that we are not somehow desecrating His abode by examining nature. God is at work within creation (in that sense He is immanent and transcendent at the same time).

28. Since God is rational, we can expect that, even in its fallen state, the universe contains rational laws and, even in our fallen state, our reason is attuned to discovering those laws. Here it is important that our reason is like the reason in nature, because the two have a common source in God. Although "[His] ways are higher than [our] ways" (Isaiah 55:9) and there are mysteries of faith we cannot fathom, we are equipped to understand much about how God's world works.

29. Allegories encourage one to indulge in endless speculation about what things might be for, distracting one from the more basic scientific task of finding out what caused them and how they work.

30. A literal approach focuses science on accurate description and measurement. This allows precise predictions, testing, and an increasing ability to control and regulate phenomena. Facts are not everything in science, but they do form the database that a scientific theory attempts to explain, and the more accurate the facts, the more scientists can conform their theories to reality.

31. This tells us that nature is more like a book than a cake. In a cake, various elements are stirred together randomly in an appeal-

ing form, which nonetheless does not say anything. A book, however, contains specifically arranged information that derives from an author's mind and communicates to the book's reader.

The speech of the natural world consists in part of the mathematical regularities that govern its operation, and which can be "read" by highly trained scientific minds. Scientists are encouraged to believe that such regularity exists to be discovered, and hence that the search for regularity is not a waste of time, as it would be if chaos was the ultimate reality.

32. People often cannot see God's work in nature because sin makes them turn away from God in enmity. Unrepentant sinners then seek to suppress the truth that they really know; they deceive themselves by exchanging truth for more comforting lies. It is not that unrepentant people cannot see God's work in nature, but that they will not see it.

33. If scientists see themselves as priests, they know that they serve in a temple built by someone much greater than themselves. They cannot expect to acquire infallible and ultimate knowledge, but they can be confident that God has provided a meaningful "text" in nature that we are able to read. The idea of "thinking God's thoughts after Him" reminds us that some of God's thoughts are higher than our thoughts; nonetheless, there are coherent truths to discover.

34. Islam insists that Allah is entirely other than us, that he would not and could not be like us, and so there is no "middle man," such as our mediator, Jesus Christ. This view raises a very serious problem of how such a god can communicate with human beings at all. And even if he did, how could we know it, if anything such a god said transcended our powers of understanding? Why suppose that such a god cares about human beings in particular, when he has done nothing to identify with their affliction?

Christianity comforts us because it tells us that God became man to identify with our suffering, to show that He meant to save us, and to present God in a form we can relate to and understand.

35. The priesthood of science is simply a priesthood of one vocation among many. No special honors are conferred on scientists by God; they simply take their place with all other vocations. And no matter how often they succeed, scientists can save no one by their work. By contrast, Jesus is a high priest who sacrificed Himself once and for all to pay the price for all sin and to save us all. Scientists can be comforted that they do not need to function as saviors. They are freed to imitate Christ's sacrifice by allowing their old selves to be

crucified, so that the new selves in Christ can better serve their neighbors through scientific work.

36. Scientists do not have to make the world fit together correctly. The world already fits together because it was created through Christ and is still held together by Him. This assures the scientist that there is meaning behind and beyond this world, giving work a purpose now and hope for life in eternity.

CHAPTER FOUR

Science Serves Our Neighbors

Objectives

By the power of the Holy Spirit working through God's Word, participants will see that scientists do not have an exemption from God's moral law, understand that scientists are equal members of the community (dependent on, yet able to serve others), and see that the spiritual insight that enables us to see ourselves, God, and others in a true light comes from God.

Opening Worship

Invocation

In the name of the Father, the Son, and the Holy Spirit. Amen.

Readings from God's Word

The eye cannot say to the hand, "I don't need you!" And the head cannot say to the feet, "I don't need you!" 1 Corinthians 12:21

Instead, speaking the truth in love, we will in all things grow up into Him who is the Head, that is, Christ. From Him the whole body, joined and held together by every supporting ligament, grows and builds itself up in love, as each part does its work. Ephesians 4:15–16

Opening Prayer

Lord, Heavenly Father, through Your Son You

reconciled the world to Yourself. Draw all of us, including scientists, to be reconciled to one another in the body of Christ, so that together we may serve as we have been served. Amen.

37. Answers may vary.

38. Most vocations are offices instituted by God through the order of creation and preservation. As a result, they fall under the "left hand" kingdom of God's Law. The fact that the content of scientific theories is devoid of morality does not make scientific office holders exempt from God's moral law, anymore than accountants stop being human beings or citizens because they only study numbers. In a community, we must be concerned about how our work is used by others. Scientists are called to work with others to help their neighbors, and they are not doing that if their results are being used to harm others.

39. All human beings are called to be stewards of their natural environment. Scientists have a special responsibility because they understand better than nonscientists how that environment works and because they can control and adapt it for good and bad purposes. Nature is not to be worshiped, as if it is a god, or to be trashed, as if God had not made it. Nature has value in its own right as part of God's creation and value for human beings as a precious resource to be husbanded.

Gardeners do not leave nature to its own devices or exterminate all life to make a pavement. They nurture living things and use them to provide food for our bodies and beauty for our eyes. Likewise scientists intervene in nature, but should do so to meet needs and beautify the environment, not to despoil it.

40. Answers may vary. Scientists may be tempted to see an unfortunate human being as a way of testing a hypothesis, even without that person's knowledge or consent. Should unwitting humans be exposed to the fallout from a nuclear bomb test to see what the effects of radiation might be on human beings? Should a patient who might recover from a disease in a few years without treatment be an involuntary guinea pig for any and every medicine designed to accelerate recovery? When human beings are treated as no more than experimental subjects, the personal is reduced to the impersonal and human dignity is violated.

41. Answers will vary. Ethical science has produced countless devices that help disabled people function more effectively by compensating for weakened, broken, and unresponsive limbs. Our

sight and hearing is much improved, ligaments are replaced, and prosthetic limbs extend our control. Voluntary subjects courageously try new drugs that may lead to important cures for serious diseases. New scopes, cameras, and lasers allow specialized operations with an accuracy and safety level undreamt of only 20 years ago. All of these advances help people continue in productive work and help them to enjoy the life God gave them.

42. In a body, all the parts are interdependent. There is no use having a brain without a heart to pump blood to the brain or lungs to provide oxygen to be transported by the blood. Likewise, scientists have a role to play only in relation to others. Some may regard scientists as the brains of society, but scientists rely on others to bring them raw materials for their experiments and to provide the food, housing, clothing, and transportation that science has helped to improve. They rely on sound government, which protects all legitimate callings through law enforcement and the military. And scientists would be useless if there were no other people who benefited from their results or who could use their results to serve still others.

43. In our modern age, scientists seem to stand out because of their specialized knowledge and power. They can seem like secular magicians who can do things other people cannot. When it comes to plumbing and building, however, the average theoretical physicist or organic chemist is no better off than the average postal worker. Such a person relies, or is well advised to rely, on the vocations of plumber, architect, and construction worker. We need constantly to remind ourselves that specialized knowledge in one area is not godlike knowledge of all areas.

44. Many computer users complain that computer scientists spend too much of their time developing flashy features and too little on improving reliability, security, and ease of use. The pharmaceutical industry also produces an inordinate number of drugs for mental and physical conditions that might be remedied by alternate means (e.g., diet and exercise). These drugs often have side effects at least as bad as the original ailment, and are clearly over-marketed and over-prescribed. As a result, many people end up taking drugs they do not need and in combination with other drugs, which may lead to dangerous interactions. Scientists who pander to the consumer society's insatiable desire for quick fixes do not serve the needs of their neighbors, but tell them what their "itching ears want to hear" (2 Timothy 4:3). A most tragic case is the over-prescription of Ritalin for unruly children, which evades serious questions about whether parental neglect

and abuse is the real problem in some of the cases. There may also be health risks from children taking such drugs for a protracted period of time.

Scientists can refocus their work by remembering that they should be most concerned to provide for their neighbors' needs, not their wants. They should also see their primary goal as supporting existing and useful vocations, rather than further weakening them by providing a scientific surrogate.

45. Science does provide intellectual enlightenment. But reason does not save, and intelligence in the service of greed, ambition, pride, and arrogance only exacerbates evil by making it more potent. The spiritual enlightenment, which shows us our true condition, makes us depend on God, and the desire to serve others in humility only comes from God, not our autonomous intellectual development.

46. Legal restraint curbs our selfish desires only because we want to be rewarded for good behavior or to avoid punishment for bad behavior. Such "enlightened self-interest" helps keep order, but if a scientist believes he or she can benefit from unethical behavior that won't be detected, what will hold that person back? Conscience may help, but conscience is corrupt since the fall and we engage in all sorts of self-deception to suppress it.

The Gospel provides a sense of gratitude and love of neighbor that makes us want to do the right thing. Christians—scientists or otherwise—no longer see themselves as special or others as inferior, but seek to do what they can to hold the body of Christ together and to draw others to it.

CHAPTER FIVE

Science, Beauty, and God's Handiwork

Objectives

By the power of the Holy Spirit working through God's Word, participants will see why reductionism fails to explain the true, the good, and the beautiful, understand how our Beautiful Savior works despite the ugliness of sin, and see the beauty of Christ hidden in the ugly affliction of those who need our love.

Opening Worship

Invocation

In the name of the Father; His Son, our Beautiful Savior; and the Holy Spirit. Amen.

Readings from God's Word

He had no beauty or majesty to attract us to Him, nothing in His appearance that we should desire Him. Isaiah 53:2b

Finally, brothers, whatever is true, whatever is noble, whatever is right, whatever is pure, whatever is lovely, whatever is admirable—if anything is excellent or praiseworthy—think about such things. Philippians 4:8

Opening Prayer

Lord, heavenly Father, forgive us for seeing only the ugliness of sin in a fallen world. Help us to see the beauty of Your guiding hand and the beautiful Savior who is Your Son, sent to save us and hidden in our neighbor. Amen.

47. Answers may vary.

48. Answers may vary. Would such a life be worth living?

49. Our prior worldview controls how we interpret facts. For example, the Cartesian mechanists thought that all causation involved the direct contact of material particles. Therefore, they initially dismissed Newton's idea of gravitation as an "occult" force that would have to work across empty space. Newtonians likewise came to see the world as a clockwork machine and were opposed to the idea of random chance, which figures so prominently in quantum mechanics. Reductionists think that everything that occurs can be reduced to the current or prior state of unaided nature.

If someone seemed dead and then alive, then the reductionist would say either that the person was not really dead, or that, although he or she was, there was some unknown natural process that brought the dead person back to life. Having dismissed the possibility of miracles, no evidence, however strong, is allowed to substantiate a miracle.

50. Cutting God out of science and life will ultimately lead to selfish self-destruction. Motivation is an essential ingredient of success. Science motivated by love for the Creator and one's neighbors will steer science in the direction of responsibility and mutual care.

51. It is odd for reductionists to claim both that design does not really exist in nature and that scientists design experiments. The reductionists view scientists as just part of nature, and so if there is no design in nature, there is none in the scientist either. But if scientists do not design experiments, then they are not really in control. They are simply passive puppets controlled by undirected processes in their brains and environment. But if that is so, it seems that science is not rational and there is no ground for expecting that it can find truth (that is, if one can still speak of something called truth). Why suppose that undirected processes that are not even looking for the truth can find it? If scientists really are as reductionism implies they are, surely this is the blind leading the blind.

On the other hand, if reductionists admit that, by some fluke, undesigned processes generated human beings who can really design things, then they are admitting that design can really exist somewhere in nature. But if that is so, why should this be the only place? If design is a legitimate scientific category, because humans design things, then there is no way to exclude the possibility that divine design is operative and detectable in nature as well.

52. If reductionism is true, beauty is an odd luxury, something we happen to like because of the way evolution happened to develop us, but with no objective basis. Reductionism cannot therefore explain the fact, admitted even by atheist scientists like Steven Weinberg, that beauty is an objective sign of truth. Christians can surely suggest that even in a fallen world God's beauty would leave behind beautiful traces, and that we would expect beautiful laws to govern His world.

53. Without the idea of truth, science degenerates into pragmatism. For example, Ptolemy's model of the solar system worked surprisingly well, so scientists could have rested content with it. But they became convinced that it was false and looked for a model that was closer to the truth. Christians who are scientists believe in an author of objective truths that are there for us to discover, and although indeed, as Karl Popper said, "truth is hard to come by," Christians who are scientists should never give up the search for it. Without goodness, science lacks proper direction and again may fall into pragmatism, aiming to please and make a profit, and willing to compromise ethics by treating some humans as "more equal than others." A focus on goodness orients the scientist to honorable research methods aimed at making other people's lives better. Without beauty, scientists can too easily accept ugly but practical solutions and fall away from a higher standard that honors God and respects creation.

54. An attitude of nihilism (the view that nothing really matters) is very dangerous in scientists since their knowledge can then serve dishonest and evil ends. Focusing on truth, scientists will want to find out even things that many people do not want to hear. For example, some scientists are investigating whether or not there is a connection between abortion and breast cancer. If indeed there is such a link, a scientist who discovered it would demonstrate real love for women, who could then reconsider their options. A focus on beauty will encourage scientists to produce results that will help those who feel ugly because of disabilities to relate effectively to others via technological aids. Such scientists would also seek to explore the natural world without gratuitous disfigurement or depletion of its resources. And because of an orientation to goodness, the work of these scientists would aim to alleviate damage, deficit, and suffering, not to cause these things.

55. Behind all appearances, no matter how ugly, is the beauty of the Word (John 1:1–3), the Creator and Preserver of all, and the

underlying rational principle that makes science possible. Behind the ugliness of paralysis, there may be a beautiful mind whose creative potential is revealed when specialized computers allow communication. Friendship, love, and faith that were always there can now be expressed and returned by others. Behind the ugliness of disease, there are beautiful structures and laws that allow scientists to understand the disease and find a cure.

56. In this fallen flesh, we can only ever have partial knowledge. Our minds are not powerful enough or clear enough for more than that. But partial knowledge is better than no knowledge. We can say that God is hidden (*Deus absconditus*) and we cannot fully know Him. Yet we can also say that God reveals Himself (*Deus revelatus*) and thereby we can know Him. Likewise with nature, we can know with confidence what God chooses to reveal to us, but are spared from the need to know everything about nature. Since what we can know is revealed by God Himself, we can be confident that it is at least a glimpse of objective truth.

57. If the world exists of itself, disconnected from God, then there is no reason to expect that there are valuable truths to discover, and the wonder and enthusiasm of science is killed. But if the Gospel opens our eyes again to God as the architect, then the universe is His temple, a place full of His marvelous works. This recreates wonder and draws the mind to look for the higher things of God as evidenced in nature. Openness to truth, goodness, and beauty has led scientists to more accurate, more helpful, and more elegant and simple theories of the universe.

58. Answers may vary. The more scientists succumb to materialism, the more they tend to hold a self-contradictory view, according to which scientists should be exalted for having the specialized knowledge that human life is meaningless. Obviously, if human life is meaningless, this applies to scientists as well, and there is no basis for exalting them.

Seeing oneself and others as redeemed by Christ restores a sense of value for all human beings while denying any exalted value to oneself—even if one is a scientist. Scientists who are Christians see others as beautiful for just the same reason they are, because Christ has honored them by bestowing His righteousness on them. Such scientists are now focused on reflecting that beauty in their treatment of others. The practical result is a more other-centered, sacrificial life.

CHAPTER SIX

Defending the Faith with Science

Objectives

By the power of the Holy Spirit working through God's Word, participants will understand that although apologetics saves no one, it can help an unbelieving neighbor overcome obstacles to the faith, see that modern science provides powerful arguments for a divine being, and understand how Christianity succeeds where other religions fail, in making this divine being personally known to us through Christ.

Opening Worship

Invocation

In the name of the Father; His Son, the Logos, in whom all things hold together; and the Holy Spirit. Amen.

Readings from God's Word

But in your hearts set apart Christ as Lord. Always be prepared to give an answer to everyone who asks you to give the reason for the hope that you have. But do this with gentleness and respect. 1 Peter 3:15

Philip said, "Lord, show us the Father and that will be enough for us." Jesus answered: "Don't you know Me, Philip, even after I have been among you such a long time? Anyone who has seen Me has seen the Father." John 14:8–9

Opening Prayer

Lord, Heavenly Father, send Your Spirit to loosen our tongues that we may humbly defend Your ways, not because You need it, but because our neighbors may benefit from hearing the reason for the hope that is within us. Never let us forget, though, that our own reasoning skills save no one and that we depend entirely on faith born of grace. Amen.

59. Twentieth-century Germany illustrated many of the worst results of secularization. This was epitomized in the rise of Nazism, which stepped into the spiritual and cultural vacuum created by secularization.

60. Laws are ordinances that govern how things are done. But of course laws imply the existence of a lawgiver! Laws tell us how things are supposed to go, and therefore invite the question "Supposed by whom?" A secular understanding of science excludes a divine lawgiver and so undermines any basis for saying that natural regularities are laws. There is no justification for calling these regularities laws if no one laid them down. The whole idea of a law of nature really derives from the theological doctrine of providence.

61. Science alone does not provide meaning, even at the most basic level of deciding how science should be used. Without the doctrine of vocation, science is just an applied rational activity whose results can be used for any purpose whatever. At a deeper level, science can remedy problems, but it cannot cure sin, conquer death, or save anyone. Christianity gives meaning for this life, directing us to serve others. Ultimately it gives meaning beyond this life, in eternal communion with God.

62. Answers will vary. Suppose you are walking in South Dakota. You see some interesting angular rocks that vaguely resemble a human head, but realize that they are not very complex or specific and could have formed either by random wind action (chance) or by a freeze-thaw cycle (law). A little while later, however, you see Mount Rushmore, with the faces of American presidents carved in its rock. You can be quite certain that an effect of this complexity and specificity, matching the appearance of independently identifiable human beings, did not arise from mere chance or natural law. In this case, it is reasonable to conclude that human agents intervened to design a

product that unaided nature would not have produced.

Now suppose a scientist discovers that all life contains extremely complex, tightly specified information, and can argue rigorously that this cannot have arisen by chance or law, and that there were no intelligent, finite agents around to produce it. Then it is reasonable to conclude that the information derived from supernatural agency. The same argument can be made for the simplicity of the fundamental laws of nature and the fine-tuning of the cosmological constants for life.

63. Rational order is objectively in the creation through Christ, even behind apparent chaos. This is because our own minds are shaped by Him; thus we are equipped to discern that order. The scientific search for laws of nature is thus on firm ground. For an atheist, however, there is no God and no ground for believing that such rational order exists. What is more, even if it did exist, there is still no warrant for supposing that we are equipped to detect it.

64. Scientists know how to investigate difficult problems, marshal their evidence, and build convincing arguments and explanations. Christians who are scientists can take these abilities and use them to show how science points to God.

65. The apostle Paul states that God created the world and the human race "so that men would seek Him and perhaps reach out for Him and find Him" (v. 27). Through preachers "He commands all people everywhere to repent" (v. 30). He raised Christ from the dead since "He will judge the world with justice by the man [Jesus] He has appointed" (v. 31). Theologians, can there be any doubt that God wants to communicate with us?

66. Anyone can be an apologist, even those who are equipped only with their personal confession of faith and not intellectual arguments. For apologists to be really effective, they should learn to defer to the expertise of those who have the relevant vocation. We can be happy to appeal to historians, legal scholars, philosophers, theologians, and scientists when they have the gifts to defend the faith. We are not saved by our defense and do not have to work out all the details on our own. And even if we feel incapable of defending the faith, we can simply point to others in the body of Christ who are better equipped.

67. Answers will vary. Although apologetics is not the same as evangelism (presenting the Gospel), the Gospel is the end the apologist should have in view. Master apologist Ravi Zacharias uses an old

Indian proverb to make the point that we should not cut off a person's nose and then ask him to smell the rose of the Gospel. If we "win" an argument by humiliating someone, we may only alienate that person from Christianity and create a wounded pride that will reject the Gospel. Better than confronting people in this fashion is standing side by side with them and showing them respectfully the grounds for Christian claims. It may take time. But ultimately, it is God, not us, who grants the increase of faith.

68. If Shakespeare is the author, but stays entirely out of the play and does not even include lines that point to him, then a character in the play, such as Hamlet, has no way of knowing the author. Indeed the play may not have an author, but may be like improvisational theatre, "a tale told by an idiot, full of sound and fury, signifying nothing" (*Macbeth*, Act 5, scene 5). If we are like Hamlet in such a play we cannot know God or be saved from our predicament.

But in the drama of this world written by God, the Author of life also writes Himself in as a character in the play and comes to dwell among us. Just as Alfred Hitchcock often appeared in his own movies, so our God appeared so that we may know Him through the person of Christ. Most scandalously of all, this all happened in the same grimy history that we all inhabit. Here Christians have a solid basis for their faith, the likes of which is completely lacking in other religions. Either these other religions have no historical basis at all, or if they do, they provide no grounds for supposing that God has spoken to us and for us. Our God humbled Himself to become man and to die on a cross for our sins for that very purpose.

Appendix on Evolution

It is often confidently asserted today that large-scale evolution is no longer simply a theory, but a fact, so that disagreeing with evolution is like denying that the earth is round. However, an increasing number of scientists and philosophers argue that these claims go far beyond what the evidence actually warrants, and they also point out that strong evidence points in the opposite direction.

The "evolution" we can actually observe is so-called microevolution, where there is an increase in the frequency of some members of a species due to a change in environmental conditions. For example, bacteria that are resistant to antibiotics become more predominate than those that are not. Insects respond in a similar way to insecticides. However, when the antibiotics or insecticides are removed, the populations return to normal, with the same distribution of characteristics they had before. And, most important, there is no evidence that these changes in the distribution of characteristics within the population ever produce a new morphology (or body plan), which is required for a new species to form. In other words, microevolution does not provide a plausible account of macroevolution. (For more details, see Michael Denton's Evolution: *A Theory in Crisis* [Adler & Adler, 1985], Phillip Johnson's *Darwin on Trial* [National Book Network, 1991], and Jonathan Wells's *Icons of Evolution* [National Book Network, 2000].)

In addition, Darwin's theory claims that evolutionary change is undirected and the result of chance and therefore can be predicted to be gradual. If this is correct, then, as Darwin himself admitted, there should be innumerable transitional forms in the fossil record. Yet they are not to be found, as even the noted paleontologist and evolutionist Stephen Jay Gould admitted.

Finally, in his book *Darwin's Black Box* (Free Press, 1996), Michael Behe has argued that there is a good reason why a gradual Darwinian path cannot explain certain biological structures: they are irreducibly complex. What this means is that like the common household mousetrap, many biological structures have a number of well-matched parts, the removal of any one of which would prevent the system from functioning. It is hard to see how such structures could develop gradually, since the simpler precursor systems do not work and so would not be selected. Darwinists have proposed "indirect scenarios" to overcome this difficulty, but these do not work either (see William Dembski, *No Free Lunch* [Rowman & Littlefield, 2002], chapter 5, and Angus Menuge, *Agents under Fire* [Rowman & Littlefield, 2004], chapter 4).

In cases of legitimate controversy, scientists should claim only that they have a working hypothesis that covers the data in a limited domain (microevolution) and allow the evidence for and against any larger claims to be freely debated. They also should not assert that it is science that establishes philosophical views when in fact these views were really adopted prior to scientific investigation.

Glossary

allegorical interpretation. The interpretation of things or events as symbols for higher realities or truths. Allegory often denies or ignores the literal meaning of a text or a subject of study.

amoral science. The view that scientific investigation should not be obstructed by moral considerations.

apologetics. From the Greek word for "defense." The reasonable defense of one's beliefs.

autonomy. The ability to govern or control one's self.

beauty. A quality or union of qualities, such as symmetry and balance, that brings pleasure to the senses.

calling. See "vocation."

cultural mandate. God's command to Adam and Eve to cultivate and care for the garden of Eden and all creation (Genesis 1:28; 2:15).

determinism. The belief that everything happens because of causes outside of an individual. In other words, people do not have the will to make choices. What they do is caused by God, nature, society, or some other force.

empirical. Based on the senses: sight, hearing, touch, taste, and smell.

ethical science. The view that scientific investigation should be subject to and limited by moral considerations.

incarnation. From Latin, "in the flesh." It refers to the conception of Jesus in the womb of Mary by the Holy Spirit. Do not confuse *incarnation* with *reincarnation*, a Hindu doctrine.

laws of nature. The consistent behaviors of natural things, discovered by observation or experimentation (e.g., the law of gravity).

literal interpretation. A nonsymbolic interpretation of events or things according to natural meaning (e.g., a lamb is a lamb and not a symbol of something else).

logos. A Greek term for an idea, word, or reason. The apostle John uses this term to describe Jesus as the reason or logic of God's created order (John 1:1–18).

masks of God. Persons, institutions, or things through which God works in order to accomplish His purposes.

materialistic. Based on consideration of material reality, excluding spiritual realities.

metaphysics. Philosophical teaching that addresses the nature, origin, and understanding of reality.

methodological naturalism. To investigate things or events without considering supernatural causes.

natural knowledge of God. An understanding of God's characteristics through study of nature as His creation.

natural selection. The teaching that animals or people who are most fit to survive will most likely survive. This is also called "survival of the fittest."

original righteousness. The state of sinless perfection into which God created Adam and Eve (Genesis 1:31; 2:25).

pantheism. The philosophical position that everything that exists is god.

polytheism. Belief in multiple gods.

"priests … in … the book of nature." A name given to scientists by the astronomer and mathematician Johannes Kepler. Kepler held that scientists were God's servants (priests) studying God's creation (the book of nature).

priesthood of all believers. The belief that every Christian is called to serve God, pray to God directly, and speak God's Word (1 Peter 2:9–10).

primary creation. God's act of creating something or someone from nothing, as in Genesis 1. See also "secondary creation" and "tertiary creation."

providence. The belief that God created and continues to provide for the existence of the universe.

reductionism, materialist. The belief that the material universe has no inherent meaning; truth, goodness, and beauty are values humans impose on the material universe in their quest for meaning.

Scholasticism. From the Greek word for "school." A theological and philosophical school of late medieval Europe. Scholastics sought to prove their beliefs through logic, based on the methods of the Greek philosopher Aristotle and the citation of ancient authoritative documents such as the Bible and the church fathers.

secondary (sub) creation. The act of creating something from existing materials. See also "primary creation" and "tertiary creation."

secular salvation. The idea that science saves us by relieving us from the effects of the fall into sin (Genesis 3:15–19).

secularization. The process of eliminating theological beliefs as a basis for life and understanding.

stewardship. To act as a steward; to manage something or someone.

tertiary creation. The act of creating something by machine through programming (e.g., a computer programmed to manufacture products without direct human control). See also "primary creation" and "secondary creation."

transcendent. The teaching that God is beyond and completely separate from earthly, material reality.

utopia. An imaginary, ideal place.

vocation. The Latin word for "calling." The teaching that God calls people to certain kinds of life and work (1 Corinthians 7:17).

9 780758 600745